The effects of atmospheric pollution—Chichester Cathedral

A BIOLOGY OF MAN

VOLUME THREE
Man in Society

by

Margaret E. Hogg, B.Sc.

Head of Biology Department, I.M. Marsh College of
Physical Education, Liverpool

No man is an island, entire in itself; every man is a piece of the continent, a part of the main; if a clod be washed away by the sea, Europe is the less, as well as if a promontory were, as well as if a manor of thy friends or of thine own were; any man's death diminishes me, because I am involved in mankind. And therefore never send to know for whom the bell tolls. It tolls for thee.

JOHN DONNE
Devotions upon Emergent Occasions, 1624

HEINEMANN EDUCATIONAL BOOKS
LONDON

Heinemann Educational Books Ltd
LONDON EDINBURGH MELBOURNE AUCKLAND TORONTO
HONG KONG SINGAPORE KUALA LUMPUR
IBADAN JOHANNESBURG
LUSAKA NAIROBI NEW DELHI

ISBN 0 435 60427 9

© Margaret E. Hogg 1968
First published 1968
Reprinted 1973
Reprinted as a limp edition 1975

Published by
Heinemann Educational Books Ltd
48 Charles Street, London W1X 8AH
Printed in Great Britain by
Butler & Tanner Ltd, Frome and London

Preface

Volume Three – the last of the series *A Biology of Man* – completes the survey of man as an individual organism and as a social animal. Volume One deals with the evolution and development of the human individual and with the mechanism by which the latter is controlled; Volume Two deals with the physiological processes upon which the successful life of the individual depends, and the current volume is concerned with those factors, both genetical and environmental, which affect the normal pattern of development and activity.

Once again, as with the previous volumes, this book is intended to bridge the gap between the general texts which deal only briefly with the topics considered and the more advanced works on specific subjects. It should be useful to students in sixth forms and Colleges of Education, to student nurses and sociologists and to all whose work or interest means that they are concerned with the social aspects of human biology.

April 1968 M. E. H.

Acknowledgements

I would like once more to express my thanks to all those who have helped in the preparation of this volume, especially to Miss M. T. Crabbe, C.B.E., M.A., for her interest and encouragement and to Mr L. C. Comber, M.A., M.Sc., who again read the manuscript with great care and offered many helpful suggestions.

I am indebted to the following individuals and organisations for permission to reproduce photographs in this book:

Camera Press Limited for Plates 15, 16(a) and 16(b)
Dr D. M. Casey for Plate 12(a)
City of Bath Council for Plates 10(a) and 10(b)
National Society for Clean Air for Frontispiece
Oxfam for Plates 13(a), 13(b) and 14
Dr Peter Pearson for Plate 12(b)
Radio Times-Hulton Picture Library for Plates 2(a) and 6(a)
St Mary's Hospital Medical School for Plates 5(a), 5(b), 5(c), 8(a) and 8(b)
United Dairies for Plate 6(b)
Wellcome Historical Medical Museum for Plates 1(a) and 2(b)
World Health Organisation for Plates 1(b), 3(a), 3(b), 4, 9(a) and 9(b)

Finally I would once more like to thank the publishers, Heinemann Educational Books Ltd, for their unfailing courtesy, patience and consideration at all stages of production.

Contents

                                                                                     PAGE

I Man and his Health   I

Disease in history – Plague: a very old disease – Typhus: a war-time scourge – Smallpox: the story of vaccination – Cholera: the story of a disease in Europe – Yellow fever: a hope deferred – Malaria: winged death – Sleeping sickness: the scourge of Africa – Trachoma: a prevalent yet preventable disease – Influenza: epidemics and pandemics – The World Health Organisation – W.H.O. and malaria: the Thailand programme.

II The Biology of Pathogenic Organisms   38

Bacteria and bacterial infections – How bacteria harm the body – Bacterial diseases of man – Treponemes and Treponematosis – Viruses and virus infections – Viruses and tumours – Rickettsiae – The pathogenic protozoa – The trypanosomes – The parasitic worms – The intestinal flukes – The blood flukes – The tape worms

III The Control of Infection   76

The control of food- and water-borne diseases – The control of insect-borne infections – The control of venereal disease – The control of respiratory infections – Prophylaxis and artificially induced immunity – The pattern of a clinical infection – The control of diphtheria – The control of pulmonary tuberculosis – Chemotherapy – Mode of action of sulphonamides and antibiotics – The evolution of resistant strains of bacteria – The use of penicillin in the treatment of treponematoses.

IV The Biological Basis of Immunity   95

The antigen–antibody reaction – Interferon – Other important antigen–antibody reactions – Other antigen–antibody reactions – ABO blood grouping – The chemistry of the blood group antigens – Antigens and skin-graftings.

	PAGE
V Environmental Hazards to Health	108

Smog – Dust – Silicosis – Prevention of Silicosis – Asbestiosis – Pneumoconiosis of coal miners – Effects of pneumoconiosis – The cotton industry – Ionising radiation – Radiation and blood disease – Radiation and cancer – Cancer radiotherapy – Radiation during pregnancy – Pesticides – Tobacco smoking.

VI Congenital Abnormalities   126

Defects in the genetic plan – Chromosome abnormalities and leukaemia – Congenitally acquired defects – Congenital abnormalities due to the interaction of heredity and environment – The effects of prematurity – Defects caused during birth – Infection during birth.

VII Man and his Food   136

The problems of undernourishment and malnutrition – Calories needed and available – The increase needed in total food production.

VIII The Population Problem   146

The nature of the problem – The possible solutions to the problem – Control of population growth.

Index   155

List of Plates

Frontispiece

Effects of atmospheric pollution

between pages 6 and 7

Plate 1 Plague – yesterday and today
Plate 2 Smallpox and cholera – epidemic diseases of the past
Plate 3 Malaria and sleeping sickness – scourges of today
Plate 4 The W.H.O. headquarters in Geneva

between pages 38 and 39

Plate 5 Bacteria and viruses
Plate 6 The pioneer and the outcome of his work
Plate 7 Protection from tuberculosis by injection
Plate 8 Penicillin – miracle drug

between pages 70 and 71

Plate 9 Miracle drug – the effects
Plate 10 Atmospheric pollution
Plate 11 Human albinos
Plate 12 Normal and abnormal human chromosomes

between pages 142 and 143

Plate 13 Malnutrition
Plate 14 A severe case of Kwashiorkor
Plate 15 Man against the desert
Plate 16 Conquering the desert

CHAPTER I

Man and his Health

Disease in history

When the world was young and man first walked the earth the greatest problem which he had to solve was how to stay alive: life was for the strong and survival of the fittest was the greatest natural law. The all-important unit was the individual; problems of health were essentially personal. As time passed, however, man ceased to depend entirely upon hunting for his existence and turned to agriculture and a more settled way of life. As men came to live together, at first in small, but later in larger groups, many new problems inevitably arose, not least among which was the general welfare, both of individual members of the group, and of the group as a whole. Health became, and has ever since remained, the problem not only of the individual but also of the community.

As age succeeded age and society became increasingly complex, the problem of community health assumed ever widening proportions. The problem became first parochial, later national, and has now assumed global proportions. Paradoxically enough, this situation does not minimise, but serves only to accentuate, the ultimate responsibility of the individual. The health of a country depends in the long run upon that of each of its inhabitants: the secret of world health is to be found ultimately in the homes of its people.

What then is health? In the constitution of the World Health Organisation health is defined as '... a state of complete physical, mental, and social well-being and not merely the absence of disease or infirmity'. Mere absence of disease, then, does not necessarily mean health, but perfect health can never be attained while disease persists. In the search for world health, the fight against disease must continue until all conquerable forms have been vanquished.

Human disease is as old as man himself. Post-mortem studies

carried out on the bodies of Egyptian men and women which have lain for thousands of years in their tombs, preserved by the ancient custom of embalming and the warm dry African climate, show that they, like modern Africans, died of pneumonia and tuberculosis; that their bodies, like those of their present-day descendants, were invaded by the virus of the blinding disease trachoma, and the parasitic fluke of schistosomiasis. Probing back even further into the past, the archaeologist finds in the bones of prehistoric man evidence that he suffered from at least two of the diseases which are still a scourge today – rheumatoid arthritis and tuberculosis: how many more diseases affected his other tissues and organs which, unlike his bones, have not been preserved for posterity, we will never know.

For thousands of years the wise leader of men has been – and still is – one who realises the importance of the health of the community which he leads. Thousands of years ago Moses was such a leader – the children of Israel wandering in the wilderness owed not only their final attainment of the promised land but their very survival during their long search at least in part to his wise understanding. The rules for community health which he laid down have been preserved in the Old Testament books of Leviticus and Deuteronomy and still make interesting reading today: 'This is the law for all manner of plague and leprosy, and scall, and for the leprosy of a garment and of a house, and for a rising, and for a bright spot: to teach when it is unclean and when it is clean: this is the law of leprosy' (Leviticus, chapter 14, verses 54–57). Moses reaped his reward: he lived to see his people reach the land flowing with milk and honey, and the proud Egypt of the Pharaohs from which they fled passed into oblivion. Egypt has not been alone in her fall: many civilisations – in Crete, Persia, and Carthage, in Babylon, Greece, and Rome – have, throughout the ages, risen only to fall again. The pages of history books are filled with descriptions of these declines, of the troubles at home and the wars abroad which have been instrumental in bringing them about. Little is written, however, of the part which may have been played by disease in precipitating these tragedies, yet pestilence, like war and famine is, and always has been, a great destroyer of peoples; an important shaper of the course of history.

Plague: a very old disease

There is probably no disease of which this is more true than bubonic plague, which has repeatedly decimated mankind since the dawn of history. The term plague is a somewhat vague one; in the literature of the time many different diseases have been so named: some of these may have been leprosy, others malaria, or smallpox. But when sufficiently detailed descriptions of the symptoms of the disease are given in the literature – large swellings in the armpits and groin – bubonic plague is easily recognisable. The disease is spread by the rat flea; human epidemics are accompanied by widespread fatal sickness among rats – reference to this further supports the identification of the disease.

Records of the effects of bubonic plague on the course of history go back a very long way. In the first book of Samuel we read the following story: 'And the Philistines fought and Israel was smitten . . . and the Ark of the Lord was taken'. And the Philistines said 'Let the Ark of the God of Israel be carried about into Gath. And they carried the Ark of the God of Israel about thither. And it was so, that, after they had carried it about, the hand of the Lord was against the city with a very great destruction; and he smote the men of the city and they had emerods in their secret parts. . . . And the men that died not were smitten with the emerods: and the cry of the city went up to heaven.' So the Philistines sent the Ark back to the Israelites and with it they sent a trespass offering 'Images of your emerods and images of your mice which mar the land: five golden emerods and five golden mice'. Clearly the pestilence was bubonic plague.

The first recorded incidence of plague in this country was in A.D. 542 and it finally disappeared after the Great Fire of London in 1666. During the intervening years repeated epidemics of varying severity materially influenced the course of English history. The first serious recorded epidemic which affected permanently the whole pattern of English life was the Black Death of the Middle Ages. This epidemic, like many others before and since, originated in Central Asia where the wild rodents of the steppes provide a permanent reservoir of the infection. Spreading slowly at first from its point of origin, the disease reached the shores of the Black Sea by 1346, and then gaining momentum as its potential victims fled ever

Westwards in a desperate effort to escape infection, finally reached Melcombe Regis in this country in July 1348. Once in, it spread through the country like a forest fire and its ravages were terrible indeed. In some parts of the country the death rate was over 90%. Crops remained unharvested, flocks untended, famine stalked in the wake of pestilence. So great was the loss of life that throughout the country the labour force was reduced by more than half: the lords of the manors found themselves bereft of the serf peasantry upon whom their prosperity depended. Ploughmen and labourers were in great demand: for the first time they were able to dictate their own terms.

> Labourers that have no land, to live on but their hands,
> Deigned not to dine a day, on night-old worts:
> May no penny ale him pay, nor a piece of bacon
> But it be fresh flesh or fish, fried or baked,
> And that chaud and plus-chaud, for chilling of their maw,
> But he be highly-hired, else will he chide.
>
> PIERS PLOWMAN

Serfdom was virtually dead: the Black Death had hastened the end of feudalism in England.

In the sixteenth and seventeenth centuries plague was endemic and often epidemic in London as in other great European cities. In the latter half of the sixteenth and the first half of the seventeenth centuries London was devastated by six major epidemics culminating in the Great Plague of 1665 immortalised by the great authors and diarists of the day. Defoe described London as 'all in tears', Pepys describes in heartrending terms the misery which the plague had caused. Probably the most moving episode of the whole tragic time was the heroic behaviour of the people of the Derbyshire village of Eyam: of the three hundred villagers who, when plague reached them from London, cut themselves off completely from all outside contacts for a full year, two hundred and fifty-nine died. But the infection was contained and the neighbouring hamlets saved. The heroism of the Rev. William Mompesson and his parishioners is commemorated annually in the little village where they lived and died (Plate 1).

In 1666 the narrow vermin-ridden streets of London were cleansed by the Great Fire, and England was rid of epidemic plague for good, though it lingered on in endemic form for some considerable time. In Europe and Asia, however, epidemic plague persisted. The last serious outbreak in Europe was at Marseilles in 1720, but in the East the worst was yet to come. Late in the nineteenth century, plague radiated once again from the remote steppes of central Asia and the most terrible wave of all swept over much of the Old World and into the New. India, Australia, and America were all engulfed and by the end of the century over thirteen million victims had been claimed. In a smaller secondary wave in 1904 and 1905, nearly one and a half million deaths occurred in India alone.

Although during the first half of the twentieth century plague has claimed hundreds of victims in many parts of the world, there have been no major epidemics except in certain parts of India. In order to understand the reason for this decline it is necessary to know something of the cause of the disease and to understand the way in which it is spread.

Plague is caused by a bacterium. The bacteria live in the blood of many species of wild rodents all over the world and are swallowed by fleas as they feed on the rodents. If the flea later bites a man the bacteria are regurgitated into the wound made in the skin and the man may develop bubonic plague, the lymph glands becoming enlarged and painful as the bacteria spread through the body: a generalised infection results in death. There is no direct spread from man to man but a flea feeding on an infected man may spread the disease to another when it in turn bites him. If the lungs of the patient are involved, however, the disease may be spread by droplet infection and the patient so contaminated develops a rapidly fatal form of the disease, pneumonic plague.

Many different rodents have been shown to act as hosts to the plague bacterium: marmots, ground squirrels, prairie dogs, gerbils, mice, rats, cavies, rabbits, and many others – some seventy species in all – have been incriminated in different parts of the world. But by far the most dangerous animal is the black rat. This is an indoor rat which, wherever conditions are suitable, lives in close association with human beings. In mediaeval England conditions were ideal: the rat lived and bred freely in the garbage and filth in the streets and in the straw on the living-room floors. Today the rat no longer lives in association with man because conditions are no longer suitable – there has been great improvement in the standard of domestic hygiene; houses are better built, floors are no longer covered with straw, and we ourselves are less tolerant of human parasites. Furthermore the domestic black rat has very largely been ousted by the large brown rat which does not live in association with man. Now too, man can protect himself, should need arise, by immunisation and the use of DDT. He can also benefit by the use of modern drugs: sulphonamides have a certain prophylactic value and should he be so unfortunate as to contract the disease, prompt treatment with streptomycin will increase his chance of survival from twenty-five to ninety per cent. In 1962 there were only a few hundred cases of plague reported in the whole world and these were mainly in India and South America. In this country there have been no major epidemics for over three hundred years and only seventeen deaths from plague in the last sixty years, the last, that of an experimental scientist who died in 1962. Yet the bacillus has not been exterminated: it still exists in wild rodents all over the world and given the opportunity they – especially the rats – and their fleas would be able to establish themselves in association with man and once again spread the disease to him. The most effective safeguard against plague in this country is to wage unremitting war on rats by eliminating their breeding places, by rat-proofing buildings in which food and grain are stored, and by destroying rats with poison and by trapping (Plate 1(b)). The risk of introducing plague into this country is minimised by controlling all ships docking in this country after calling at ports in plague-infected countries. The ships are thoroughly deratted and as an extra precaution metal rat guards may be fixed to the hawsers to prevent any rats which may have escaped destruction from leaving the ship. The World Health Organisation publishes a weekly epidemiological record giving full details of every infected port; this record is available to the Port Health Authorities whose representatives then derat all ships from infected ports and test samples bacteriologically for plague bacteria. In Liverpool in 1963 over a thousand black rats were destroyed: none was infected with the plague bacterium.

We have come a long way since the time of the Pharaohs. To the Israelites the cause of the plague was the hand of the Lord and the only remedy was placation by a trespass offering: to us the cause is a bacterium spread from rodents to man by the bite

PLATE 1: Plague—yesterday and today

(a) Plague 1665

(b) The control of plague today—laying rat traps in India.

PLATE 2: Smallpox and cholera —epidemic diseases of the past

(a) Dr Jenner inoculates his son

(b) Cholera in Exeter 1832— destruction of clothing

PLATE 3: Malaria and sleeping sickness—scourges of today

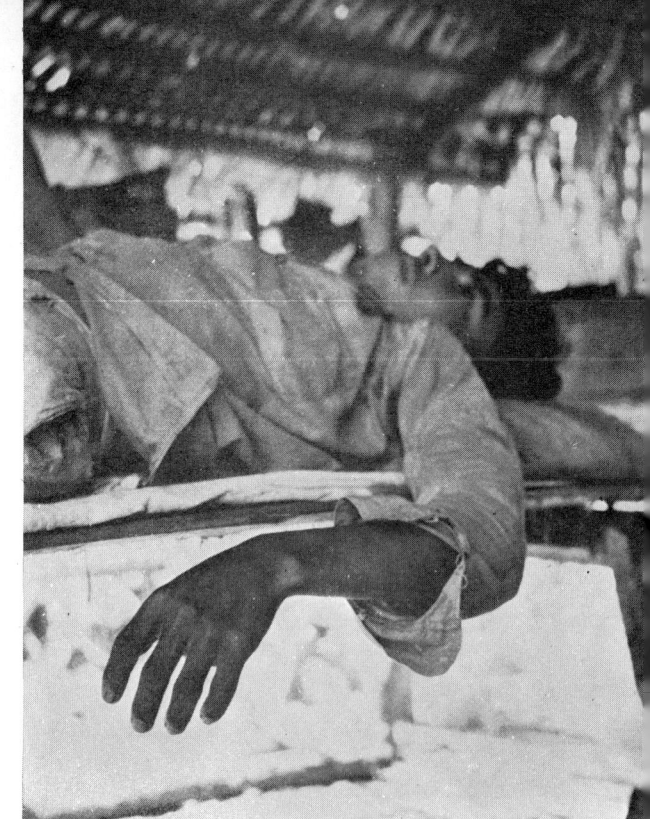

(a) A malaria patient from America

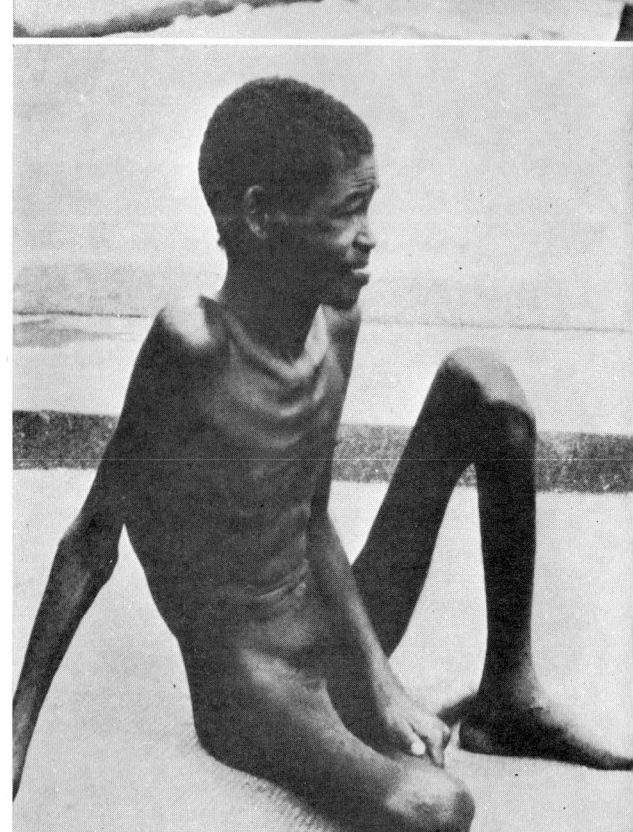

(b) A victim of sleeping sickness from the Camerouns

PLATE 4: The W.H.O. headquarters in Geneva (*background*). (The Palais des Nations is in the foreground.)

of a flea, and the sure remedy is within our grasp. But it is most important that, in our complacency, we in this country are never lulled into a false sense of security: as long as the plague bacterium and the flea-infested rat exist and as long as plague is endemic anywhere in the world, the possible danger of spread cannot be ignored. Constant, unremitting vigilance is a continued necessity.

Typhus: a war time scourge

While bubonic plague was – and is – primarily a disease of the home front, producing its disruptive effect upon the economic and social life of the country, in times of war, disaster, or famine the greatest pestilence is typhus fever. The disease is spread from man to man by the body louse, the incidence of which increases in inverse ratio to the standard of living. The lice feed only on human blood and live on man's body or in his clothing throughout their lives. They thrive best on those who wear many, heavy clothes and whose standard of personal hygiene is low. The presence of endemic typhus in the sixteenth, seventeenth, and eighteenth centuries is associated with the lousiness of the population at this time, a condition which was then regarded as undesirable but inevitable. Samuel Pepys records in his diary his disgust at the infestation of his new periwig: McArthur describes the migration of lice from the cooling body of the murdered Thomas a Becket –

... and the next day, after some debate, it was decided to remove the clothing in preparation for burial. The dead Archbishop was clad in a most extraordinary accumulation of garments. Outermost there was a large brown mantle; next a white surplice; underneath this, a fur coat of lamb's wool; then, a woollen pelisse; then another woollen pelisse; below this the black cowled robe of the Benedictine order; then, a shirt; and finally, next to the body, a tightly-fitting suit of coarse haircloth covered on the outside with linen, the first of its kind seen in England. The innumerable vermin which had infested the dead prelate were stimulated to such activity by the cold, that his haircloth garment, in the words of a chronicler, 'boiled over with them like water in a simmering cauldron', and the onlookers 'burst into alternate fits of weeping and laughter, between sorrow of having lost such a head, and the joy of having found such a saint'.

Typhus fever assumes epidemic proportions wherever men are crowded together in insanitary surroundings: throughout history these conditions have been created by war. The first epidemic ever recorded broke out in Spain when the Spaniards were fighting the Moors – the death rate from fever was nearly six times as great as that from the actual fighting – and recurrent epidemics have ever since been associated with, and often changed the course of, all major wars. The Prince of Orange making his last desperate stand to save the Holy Roman Empire from defeat by the French was saved not by his military skill but by typhus fever which decimated the besieging troops: Napoleon, trudging wearily in retreat from Moscow fought not only cold, hunger, and fatigue but also widespread fever among his already despondent troops.

The First World War was only a few months old when typhus fever reached epidemic proportions among the refugees fleeing from the battlefields of the Eastern front. Lack of contact between Eastern and Western Europe, and rigorous delousing of all prisoners from the East kept the disease out of Europe; but in post-war Russia, torn by revolution and famine, it resulted in the greatest epidemic the country has ever known – three million Russians died of typhus in the three years which followed the armistice.

In the early days of the Second World War typhus fever once again reared its ugly head, but once the campaign was thoroughly under way the danger was brought under control and no epidemic developed. This may be attributed to the greatly improved standard of living among the troops, to the availability of a suitable vaccine, but above all to the efficiency of routine delousing with DDT powder. Probably we came nearer to a major European outbreak in 1943 than at any other time. Among the million Italians crowded into war-torn Naples, devastated by Allied bombing, living in appalling, overcrowded, insanitary conditions, typhus began to find a foothold. When the Allied armies entered the city in October, an epidemic was well underway. Rigorous delousing with DDT on a scale never before envisaged brought the infection under control: by March 1944 the epidemic was virtually over.

Had the insecticidal properties of DDT been known to the Germans during the closing months of the war it is possible that at least one of the horrors which shocked the civilised world in the terrible spring of 1945 might have been averted: there might have been no typhus fever in the concentration camp at Belsen.

Typhus had reached the camp in January, brought by a trainload of Hungarian Jews moved westwards in the face of the advancing Russian armies. When the camp was liberated by the allies in April 1945 they found 20,000 typhus victims – dead and living – among the 45,000 occupants. Strict quarantine regulations combined with a mammoth delousing programme were instrumental in preventing the spread of typhus all over Europe: by May 14th the danger of an epidemic had been averted. Had DDT been used in January it might never have begun and thousands of lives might have been saved.

The control of typhus fever is self-evidently dependent upon the elimination of the body louse and the maintenance of a high standard of living. It is now possible to control the disease even under conditions of total war, provided reasonable living conditions and efficient medical control are available. Where such services are not provided typhus spreads with alarming speed, as the recent outbreak in the Congo during the troubles which followed their declaration of independence has shown. Typhus has not yet been conquered.

Smallpox: the story of vaccination

Plague and typhus have been instrumental in altering the course of history in peace and war: they have been repeatedly described in contemporary literature because of their effect on the community rather than on the individual. Smallpox when finally conquered will always be remembered with horror for its effect upon the individual himself – permanent terrible damage and hideous disfigurement leading not only to physical pain but also to the mental agony which must always accompany social ostracism. The conquest of smallpox, like that of plague and typhus, is important for man's health and happiness.

Smallpox has existed since ancient times: it is accurately described in literature as early as 1122 B.C.; it has been known for hundreds of years in Africa, Europe, and the East, and was taken to the New World by the Spanish explorers where it spread with devastating speed among the highly susceptible native Indians. The disease was virulent, the death rate high, and the aftermath terrible indeed – hideous pocks and often blindness and severe mental derangement. This highly lethal form of smallpox was widespread in England during the

Middle Ages and fortunate were those who escaped its ravages. Yet today it is no longer endemic, and it is to be its victim which causes comment. This state of affairs has been brought about by vaccination. Smallpox, unlike plague and typhus, is spread by personal contact and not by an insect vector: any direct attack upon its method of dissemination is obviously impracticable. Vaccination aims to control the disease not by preventing infection but by raising individual immunity.

The history of the control of smallpox will always be associated with the name of Edward Jenner, a man who lived a century before his time. He possessed acute powers of observation and a courage – or foolhardiness – in experimentation which today would fill us with alarm.

The story of vaccination in this country began in 1717 when Lady Mary Wortley Montague, wife of the Ambassador to Turkey, described in a letter home the Turkish practice of 'engrafting to prevent smallpox'. The operation was performed by scratching the 'venom' from a smallpox patient into a child's skin; the mild attack of the disease which followed conferred a high degree of immunity. Lady Mary had her own children engrafted; the procedure was adopted in the Royal nursery, and for fifty years it remained the standard method of smallpox control.

The fact that the mild disease of cattle – cowpox – when contracted by human beings, protected against smallpox, had long been known among west-country farmers. In 1774 a Dorset farmer, Benjamin Jetty, carried out the first true vaccination: he scratched the matter from cowpox blisters into the skin of his wife and two children. Subsequent 'engrafting' produced no sign of the disease. But the name which will always be associated with the practice of vaccination is that of Dr Edward Jenner. While still a medical student Jenner had appreciated the significance of a milkmaid's chance remark, 'I cannot take smallpox, I have had cowpox'. On May 14th, 1796, he carried out his now classic experiment: he obtained material from a cowpox blister on the hand of a dairymaid, Sarah Nelmes, and scratched it into the skin of an eight-year-old boy, James Phipps. A local reaction followed but the boy experienced no other symptoms. Jenner then inoculated into the boy, on two separate occasions, material taken from a pustule of a smallpox patient. The

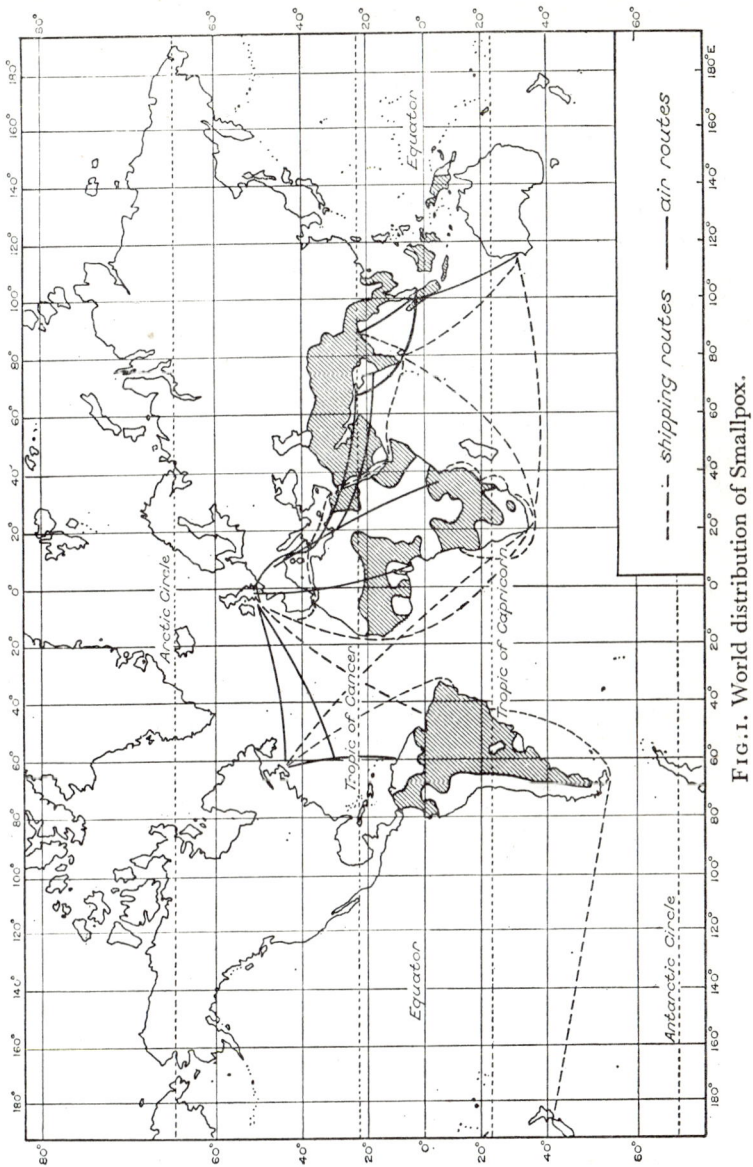

Fig. 1. World distribution of Smallpox.

boy remained perfectly healthy. Finally he inoculated smallpox material into ten people who had had cowpox: all remained healthy. The practice of vaccination had begun (Plate 2).

By 1802 Jenner's fame was fully established, not only in Britain where vaccination became compulsory, but in many other parts of the world: on July 8th, 1800, the first vaccination was carried out in America by the Professor of Medicine at Harvard Medical School who vaccinated his five-year-old son. In the late nineteenth century over 95% of the population in Britain were vaccinated, and in 1935 smallpox ceased to be an endemic disease in Britain. Today, however, now that vaccination is no longer compulsory, the percentage of those vaccinated has fallen to under thirty. Whether or not such a low acceptance of vaccination is safe is a matter of doubt: there is considerable evidence that smallpox is now occurring with increasing frequency in this country. The outbreaks are usually traceable to the importation of infected personnel from the East, an ever-increasing risk as travelling times are repeatedly reduced by the increasing speed of air travel. It is evident that we cannot afford to be complacent. Smallpox is still found in India, Pakistan, Burma, Indo-China, South America, Mexico, and parts of Africa: the flying time from these countries is less than the twelve-day incubation period of the disease (Fig. 1). The only safe remedy is world-wide vaccination. The World Health Organisation is now planning a concerted attack upon the disease in the hope that by such a global effort it can be eliminated from those countries where it is still endemic.

In recent years it has been found that a derivative of the group of chemical compounds, the thiosemicarbazones, known as methisazone, is highly active against the smallpox virus. It may prove useful in halting the infection in suspected cases, because, whereas vaccination takes from seven to ten days to give immunity, the drug provides immediate protection. What part the drug will play in world-wide eradication is uncertain, but it will without doubt be a powerful new ally to vaccination.

Cholera: the story of a disease in Europe

Many diseases have been driven from Europe through the efforts of man, through natural events, or through both. The early history of the disease is often unknown, the date of its first appearance in Europe uncertain, its life-story often undocumented. To this, the story of cholera is a marked exception: its whole history in Europe is fully recorded and contained within the span of one hundred years. A brief survey of this history follows: the story of the birth, growth, decline, and death of a disease in Europe. The information comes from the extensive studies of Dr Jacques May.

Cholera is caused by a bacterium. The faeces of the patient are heavily loaded with the organism: transmission to another individual is usually by means of infected drinking water. Food may also be involved and flies are almost certainly important as transmitting agents.

The control of the infection obviously depends upon the fact that infection only takes place when organisms from the faeces are transferred to the mouth usually by drinking water, less often by food, milk, or fingers. Water purification and adequate sewage disposal are obviously of primary importance.

Since the beginning of recorded history cholera has been endemic in India, and until 1816 it was confined to that country. In three great waves, between 1816 and 1823, between 1826 and 1827, and between 1842 and 1862, it spread first through Asia and then west to the Mediterranean, south-west to the east coast of Africa, all over Europe, and into North America (Fig. 2). 1832, 1848, and 1854 were years of fearful epidemics in England: in the Soho district of London alone 500 people died in ten days in August 1848. The fourth great wave swept through Europe between 1865 and 1875, but in this country its course was very different. The role of contaminated drinking water in spreading the disease was now appreciated (see below) and the disease had begun to be brought under control. By 1911 it was out of Europe – and kept out by stringent quarantine regulations. A final flare-up in Egypt in 1947 caused some 20,500 deaths, but now the disease is back to its pre-1816 distribution, prevented from spreading by immunisation and quarantine.

The name which will always be associated with the elimination of cholera in England is that of Dr John Snow. John Snow was born in Yorkshire in 1813 and qualified in medicine at the Westminster Hospital in 1838. As an anaesthetist he attended at the birth of several of Queen Victoria's children. Dr Snow was the first man to demonstrate the spread of a

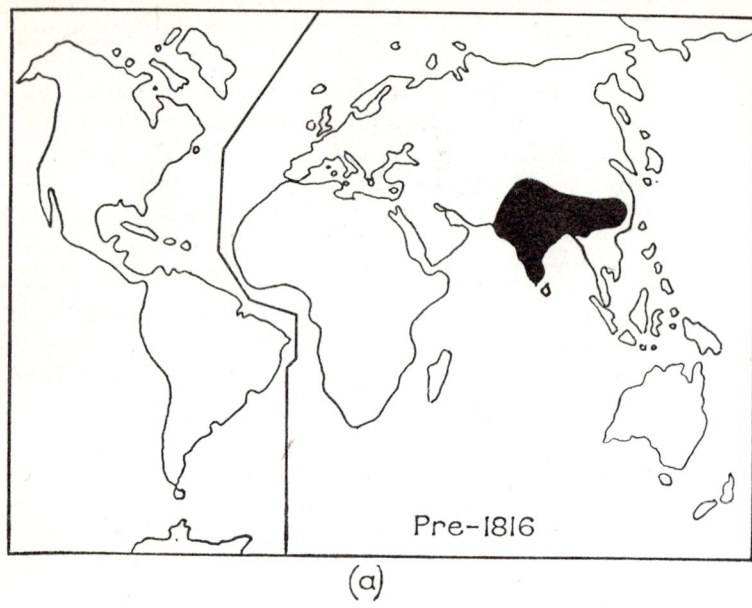

(a)

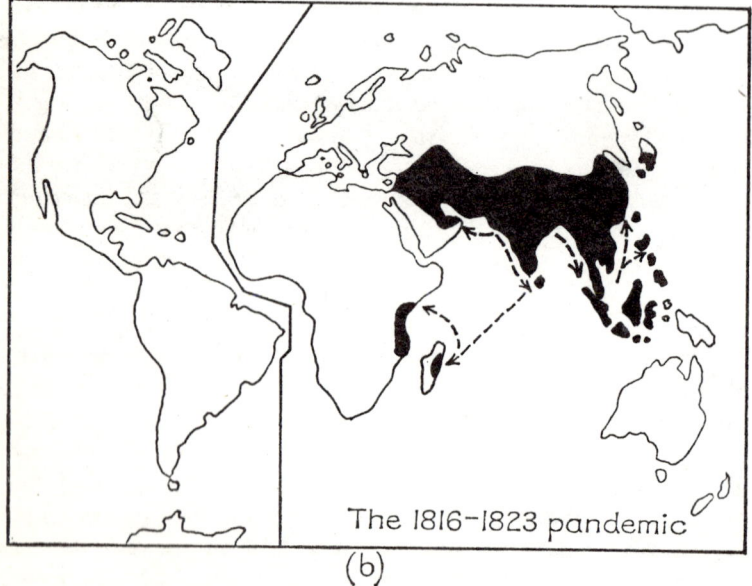

(b)

Fig. 2. The Cholera waves (Oxford projection).

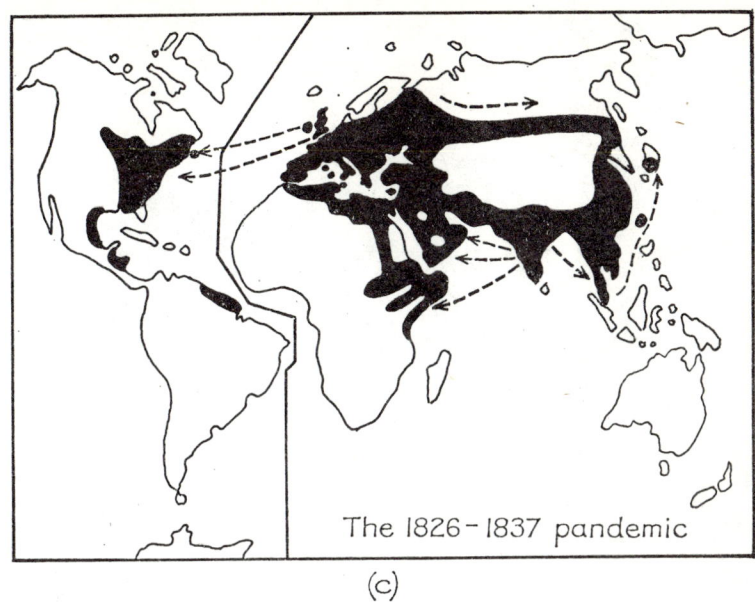

(c) The 1826-1837 pandemic

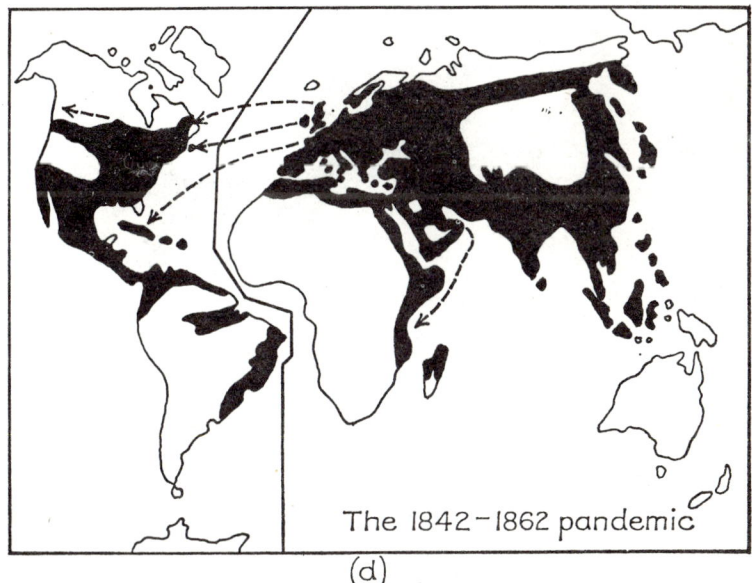

(d) The 1842-1862 pandemic

Fig. 2. (*Continued*)

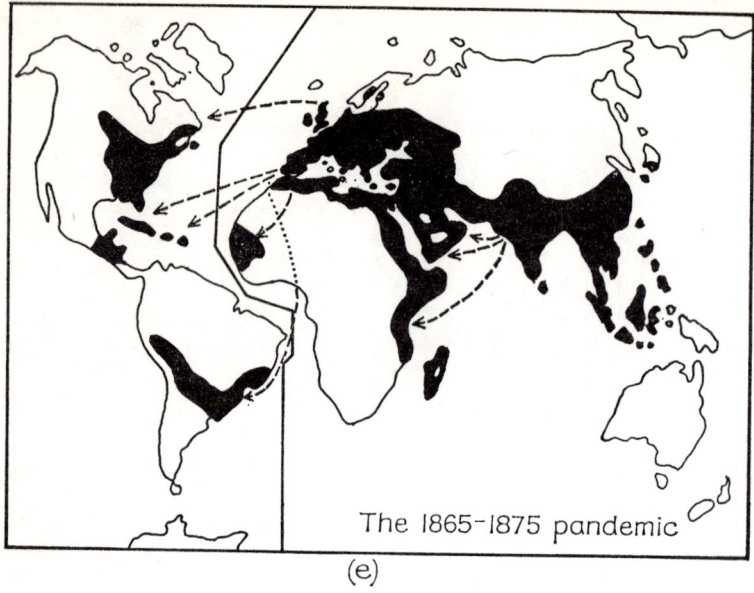

(e) The 1865–1875 pandemic

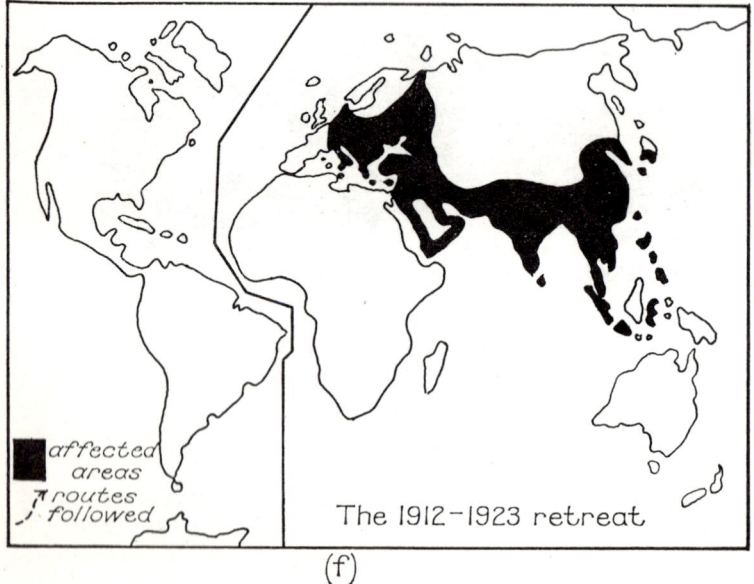

(f) The 1912–1923 retreat

affected areas
routes followed

FIG. 2. (*Continued*)

water-borne disease by contamination of the water supply by the faecal matter from an infected patient. He made an extensive study of an outbreak of cholera in the Soho district of London which began on August 31st, 1854, and resulted in 618 deaths. By painstaking enquiry and brilliant scientific deduction Dr Snow incriminated a certain pump in Broad Street. The observations on which he based his conclusions included the following:

79 people who died on September 1st and 2nd all drank water from the pump.
Two visitors to the area died: one drank water from the pump at a local restaurant, the other at the home of his brother.
A Hampstead lady who drank water from the pump, which she fetched in a bottle because she thought it was good for her, died; so did her niece who was staying with her.
Of 97 people in the area who escaped cholera, 87 did not drink the water from the pump; the other 10 drank very little.
70 employees at a local brewery either drank beer or water from a well in the brewery—none contracted the disease.
In one of two factories which had its own well there were no deaths; 7 of the 9 employees at the other factory which took its water from the Broad Street well died, the other 2 were ill.

On September 8th, on Dr Snow's advice, the handle of the suspected pump was removed and after this the epidemic soon ended. Subsequent investigation showed that the shallow well from which the pump raised the water was heavily contaminated with faecal matter from faulty sewers and cess pools: on August 28th a baby at number 40 Broad Street had contracted cholera – from what source is uncertain – and the water in which the soiled napkins were washed reached the well from the leaking cess pool.

As a direct outcome of Dr Snow's findings a Committee of Inquiry was established to investigate the outbreak, and as a result towns all over the country improved their water supply. A public house, the Dr John Snow, now stands on the site of the old pump in Broad Street, now Broadwick Street, Soho: the water – or beer – may now be drunk here, as elsewhere, in perfect safety. Efficient systems of sewage disposal and a filtered, chlorinated piped water supply keep it this way.

Yellow fever: a hope deferred

Plague, typhus, smallpox, and cholera are diseases which are part of the history of the Old World: yellow fever is integrally bound up with that of the New. No disease has had more money spent upon its elimination, none has taken a higher toll of its investigators, no story of conquest is more drama-ridden. Like plague and typhus the disease is spread from man to man by an insect vector, in this case the mosquito.

Yellow fever probably originated in West Africa where it has little effect on the natives who appear to have become immune, but it played havoc with the European settlers, and contributed greatly to the naming of West Africa as the White Man's Grave. The disease was spread to the New World by colonisation and the slave trade. On one occasion at least, in 1865, it reached England in a ship which had called at Cuba.

The disease has had far-reaching historical effects. It had much to do with the defeat of the French in the West Indies during the Napoleonic wars, and it delayed the building of the Panama Canal. The first attempt at building the canal by Ferdinand de Lesseps, who successfully built the Suez Canal, was abandoned in 1876 because of the enormous loss of life among the workmen, and it was not until 1905–6, after the discovery of the method by which the disease is spread, that the project was successfully carried out by General Gorgas.

Present-day knowledge of the nature of yellow fever and its method of transmission is largely the result of the work of two bodies of men – a Commission of the United States Army set up in 1900, which included in its personnel the well-known doctors Reid, Carroll, Agramonte, and Lazaer – and the International Health Division of the Rockefeller Foundation which studied the disease in West Africa some twenty five years later. By 1930 the pattern of transmission of the disease was well understood, the vector mosquito, Aedes aegypti, had been identified and vigorous measures adopted to bring about its eradication. By 1931 the causative virus had been identified and a vaccine had been developed. Then in 1932 came a major setback – an epidemic of yellow fever broke out in Brazil where there are no Aedes mosquitoes, and then sporadic cases and minor epidemics were detected every year in isolated jungle areas in America. The virus responsible proved to be identical with that causing the classical yellow fever and it was found to

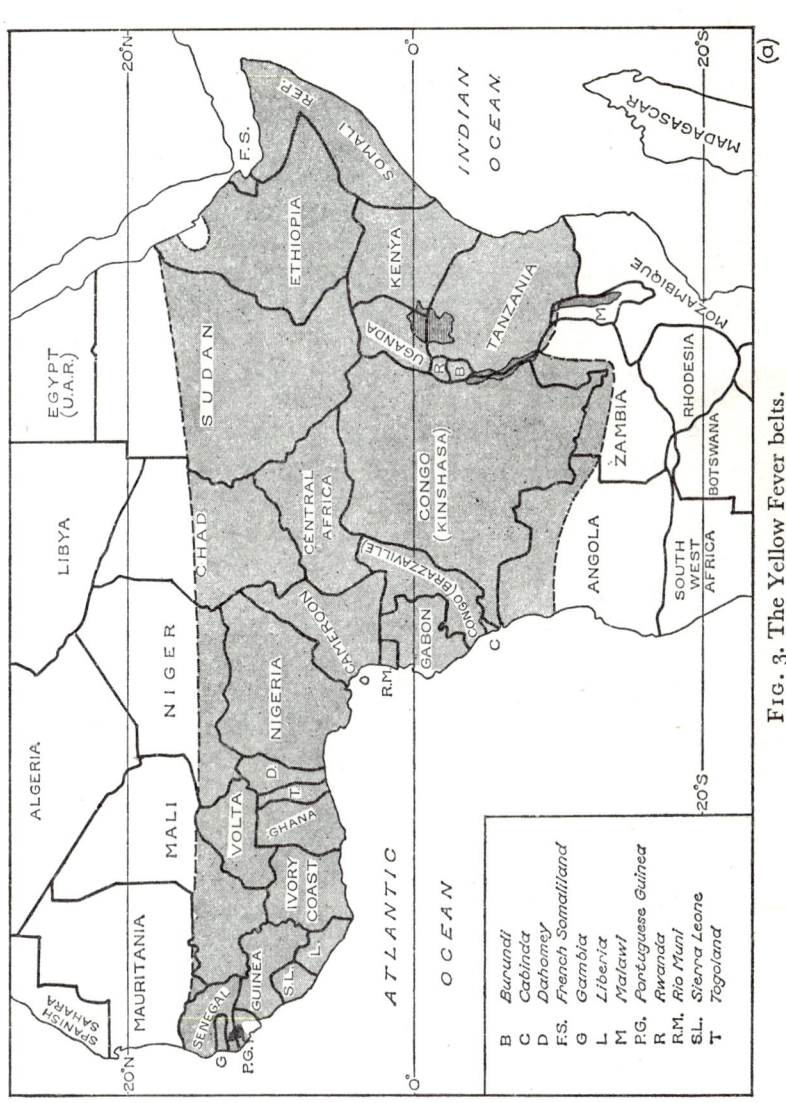

Fig. 3. The Yellow Fever belts.

live in jungle and howler monkeys and in marmosets, from which it was spread to man by different species of mosquitoes. This meant that there was an inexhaustible reservoir of the virus which could not be eradicated: total world-wide elimination of the disease from being a hope realised, became a hope deferred.

Nevertheless control of the Aedes mosquito has virtually eliminated classical yellow fever from the cities and towns where it once occurred, and the total elimination of the Aedes mosquito from the whole of the American continent is the declared objective of the Pan-American Health Organisation. The disease is now primarily one of jungle animals and is spread to human communities in rural areas by men whose work takes them into the forests. Elimination of the jungle mosquitoes is virtually impossible – the safest method of protection is by vaccination with a living attenuated virus grown in chick embryos. The distribution of the yellow fever belts where the disease still exists is shown in Figure 3. International sanitary

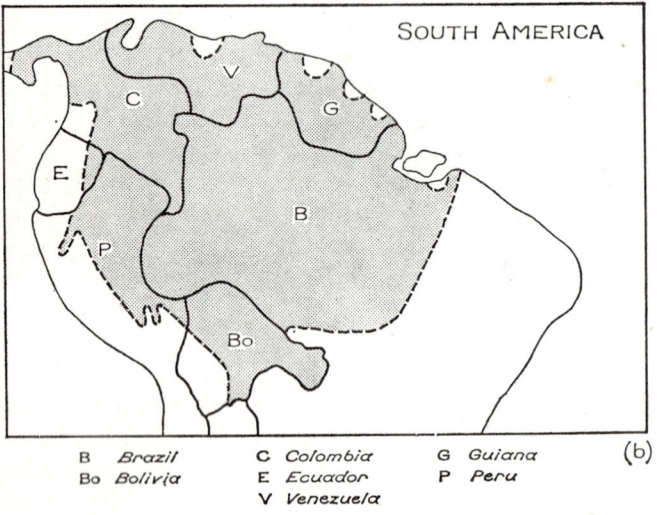

Fig. 3. (*Continued*)

agreements demand that all persons leaving by air from within any of these areas carry a current certificate of vaccination.

It will be noticed that the disease is, and always has been, absent from India, although the vector mosquito is present and the Indian monkey is highly susceptible. It is vitally important that the virus is never introduced into such a vulnerable population with so convenient an animal reservoir. The result could be disastrous.

Malaria: winged death

Malaria probably does more harm to a greater number of people than any other infectious disease: it brings sickness to some 250 million people every year, and death to two and a half million of them. Malaria, although caused by a parasitic protozoon and not by a virus, resembles yellow fever in being spread by a mosquito. It flourishes in tropical and subtropical areas all over the world, its geographical distribution being affected chiefly by the incidence of the relevant vector mosquitoes: New Zealand, Hawaii, Fiji, the Gilbert and Ellice Islands, Samoa, and the Marquesas, though lying within the possible zone, having no mosquitoes have no malaria. The mosquitoes are unable to breed at great heights and because they need water for the completion of their life cycle are absent from high and arid regions: malaria is not, therefore, a disease of the mountains and deserts. It has, however, been reported at an altitude of 9,068 feet in Bolivia and at 8,500 feet in Kenya. Malaria has also been notified as far north as 64°N at Archangel in the U.S.S.R., and as far south as 32°S in the Argentine. Intensely malarious areas include certain parts of America between latitudes 15°N and 15°S, Asia, south of latitude 40°N, Indonesia, the South-west Pacific, and many parts of Africa (Fig. 4).

Malaria is not only the cause of serious illness and death: it is also a great devitaliser of individuals and communities. It stunts development, restricts social growth, and hampers economic progress. In heavily infested areas it is the main cause of infant mortality: adults develop a considerable degree of immunity and provided they are reasonably well fed, they remain in fair condition. Where the standard of living is poor, however, as it is in many parts of India, chronic ill-health due to malaria is common (Plate 3).

The measures adopted to bring malaria under control are directed both against the adult parasites in the body of the human host, and against the mosquitoes which transmit the parasites to new victims.

Chemotherapy has long been used in the treatment of the malaria patient. By 1768, many years before the responsible organism was discovered, the anti-malarial properties of the bark of the chinchona tree were already well known. In 1820 the active principle, the alkaloid quinine, was isolated and was for many years extensively and exclusively used for prophylactic purposes. By the middle 1940's, however, modern synthetic chemotherapeutic drugs were largely replacing quinine: two, Chloroquin and Paludrine, have proved particularly effective.

The mosquitoes which spread malaria are tackled in three different ways – by drainage, by the use of larvicides, and by the use of adulticides: drainage to prevent the mosquitoes from breeding, larvicides to kill the larvae, and adulticides to kill the adult insects. Extensive drainage schemes carried out in many parts of the world have already led to the reclamation of large areas of land and the elimination of extensive mosquito breeding grounds. This method of mosquito control is, however, both expensive and uncertain: the insects breed freely not only in large sheets of water but also in small ponds and in ditches which are difficult to drain, so that mosquito elimination by this method alone is virtually impossible.

Once hatched, the larvae may be killed by the use of chemicals such as Paris green or, as they are air-breathing, smothered by oil poured onto the surface of the water. Although these methods are effective for small areas they are both expensive and impracticable for large ones and it is more usual today to direct wholesale measures not against the larvae at all but against the adult insects.

Four different adulticides have been used successfully in the war against the adult mosquito – petroleum extract of pyrethrum, dichlorodiphenyltrichloroethane (DDT), benzene hexachloride (BHC), and Dieldrin. The last three are known as residual insecticides because when sprayed onto surfaces upon which mosquitoes alight they leave a fine residual deposit which retains its lethal properties for some considerable time. One danger of continued use of DDT is already well known, the possible evolution of DDT-resistant strains. The first report of such evolution was in 1947 during experimental work with

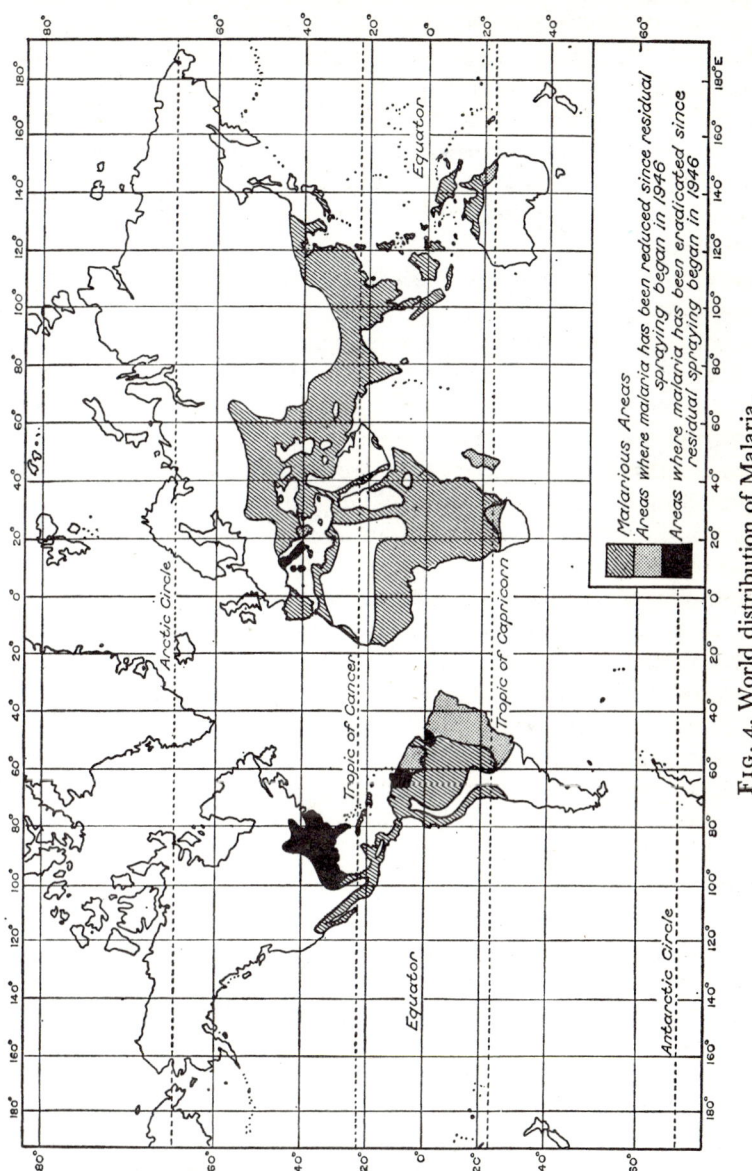

Fig. 4. World distribution of Malaria.

flies: by 1951 the first DDT-resistant strains of vector mosquitoes were reported from the U.S.A., Greece, and Panama. By 1954 it was reported from certain Greek villages and from Java that DDT spraying no longer prevented the transmission of malaria. So far there is no report of resistance to Dieldrin. The evolution of strains of mosquitoes resistant to adulticides may well prove to be a major stumbling block in the way of malaria eradication.

Sleeping sickness: the scourge of Africa

The mosquito is not the only purveyor of winged death: in an area of Africa half as large again as the whole of Australia stretching from Zululand to the Sahara, men and cattle alike are attacked by a devastating disease spread to them by the bite of a winged insect, the tse-tse fly. The disease is sleeping sickness, the causal parasite, a protozoon animal known as a trypanosome. The effect of infection on the individual is tragic, and on the community it is disastrous. The patient develops a chronic condition involving first apathy and emaciation and finally death, while in seriously affected areas the whole economy of the country is affected. Cattle die, agricultural activities suffer and vast areas of great potential value are deserted. The future development of much of the African continent waits upon the control of the disease (Plate 3).

In attempts to bring sleeping sickness under control efforts are made both to exterminate the tse-tse flies which carry the disease and, as a further precaution, to prevent infected flies from biting human beings and so transmitting the disease to them. Protection from bites is achieved by screening doors and windows, by wearing white clothing which repels the flies, by the use of chemical repellants and, as a last resort, by the removal of whole communities to areas freed from flies.

Adult flies are attacked by spraying with DDT: in large areas spraying is carried out from aeroplanes. Hand catching of flies is also practised, and is found to be effective in some areas, especially when it is combined with the clearance of the vegetation in which the flies live. Many species of flies thrive in the shady, moist conditions of densely wooded river banks and it is these river banks which are cleared. Clearing also prevents these species of flies from breeding, as the warm, moist conditions under the bark of the trees provides an ideal situation for the development of the larvae. Some species of tse-tse fly prey on wild game and destruction of the game may help in their extermination. There is, however, some disagreement about the value of this procedure and much to be said against it on aesthetic and humanitarian grounds. Overall, the most effective way of getting rid of the flies is probably clearance of vegetation.

Trachoma: a prevalent yet preventable disease

Nearly one sixth of the world's population suffer from a blinding eye disease, trachoma. The symptoms of the disease are a roughening of the conjunctiva lining the eye-lids which may spread to the cornea and cause partial or total blindness. It is a highly contagious disease and is spread by flies and water as well as by direct contact and the use of communal linen. In countries where the incidence is high, children are affected at an early age.

The disease is a very ancient one: the signs are so characteristic that descriptions in early literature are easily recognisable. A thousand years before the time of Hippocrates, the most ancient known medical treatise, the *Ebers Papyrus*, was written in Thebes: in it not only is described a disease which must have been trachoma, but also its treatment with copper. Copper sulphate is still used in the treatment of the disease today. Trachoma is endemic in many parts of Asia, Africa, Europe, and South America (Fig. 5). Some ethnic groups, especially Arabs, seem to be particularly susceptible: in the slums of Egypt over 90% of the population are affected. Although the disease is essentially one of warm countries and is especially prevalent near sea-coasts and in windy desert areas, the most important predisposing factor is a low standard of living and insanitary conditions – the major contributory factor is without doubt poverty. For this reason infection among the peoples of the under-developed countries is especially high and is a major cause of their poverty, so establishing a vicious circle. Progress in these countries depends upon this circle being broken.

As trachoma is pre-eminently a disease of poverty it could probably be eliminated by improved housing, hygiene, and nutrition. This has been the case in Finland, where a determined effort to raise the standard of living during the last fifty years has led to the total elimination of the disease which was

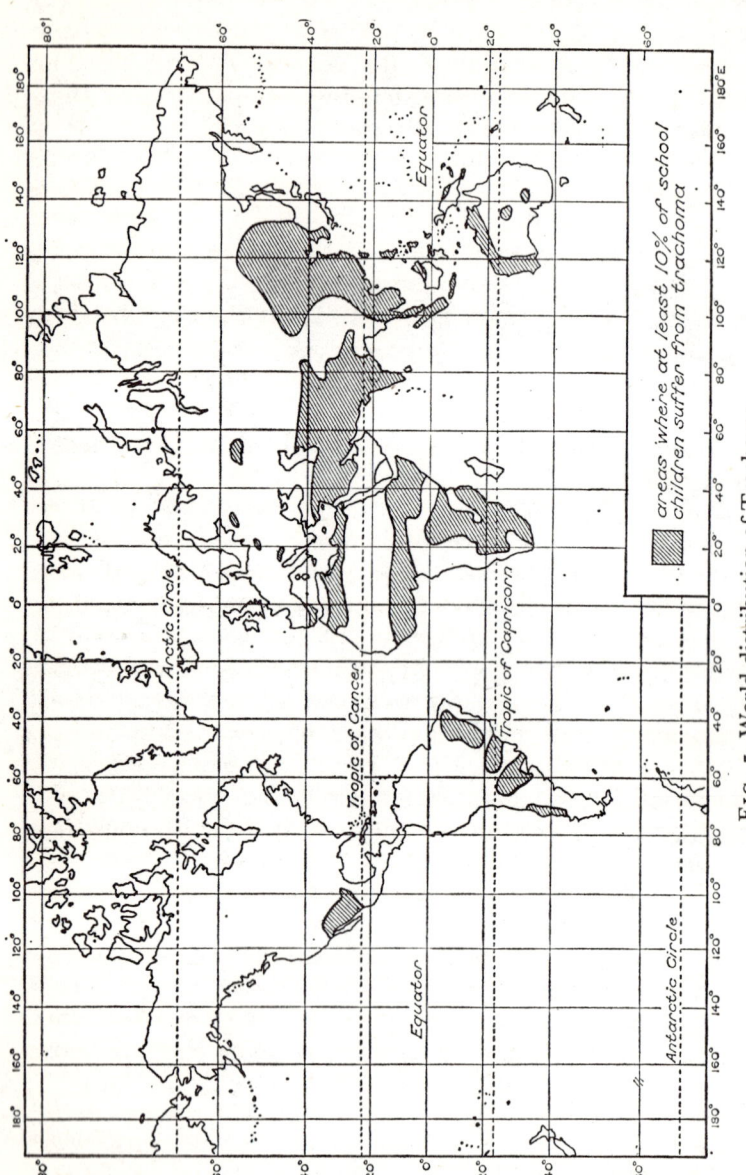

Fig. 5. World distribution of Trachoma.

previously all too common. In other parts of the world, especially in the under-developed countries, eradication by these means, though theoretically possible, still remains a practical impossibility. Two other lines of attack are, however, practicable; chemotherapy and immunisation.

Unlike the majority of virus infections trachoma responds to treatment with sulphonamides and certain antibiotics, notably aureomycin and terramycin. The sulphonamides taken through the mouth prevent the virus from multiplying; the antibiotics used as an eye lotion or ointment kill the organisms in the cells. Chemotherapy applied early on can successfully halt the progress of the disease: realisation that this is so has led W.H.O. to assist fifteen countries in extensive programmes of chemotherapeutic control. Such measures are, however, very costly and, as reinfection occurs so readily, are virtually ineffective in communities where the standard of living is low. The alternative is immunisation.

Immunisation, naturally, must await the availability of an effective, safe vaccine. The production of such a vaccine has been an incredibly difficult task for a number of reasons. The absence of any naturally occurring immunity suggests that as the infection is a local one, there is normally no antibody produced (see Chapter IV). The problem is further complicated by the existence of a large number of different strains of the virus. Appreciation of the vital importance of the production of such a vaccine has, however, added great impetus to research work and it would appear now that efforts are to be crowned with success. Animals and a limited number of human volunteers have been successfully protected – though it is not yet known for how long – by a vaccine prepared from formalin-inactivated organisms injected subcutaneously. Experiments are at present underway among Indian school children and infants in Saudi Arabia. The outlook is hopeful.

It cannot, however, be too strongly emphasised that trachoma is a disease of poverty and ignorance. An improvement in the general standard of living is still the most potent weapon of attack.

Influenza: epidemics and pandemics

In any community the infectious diseases fall naturally into two groups, the endemic, which are always present, and the non-endemic which occur in the community only on isolated occasions. The number of cases of any disease varies considerably from time to time: times of high incidence are known as epidemics. Epidemics may occur regularly or erratically: measles epidemics in London, for example, occur every two years, while those of influenza (see below) have no definite or predictable pattern. Great, wide-spread epidemics involving large areas of the world and millions of individuals are known as pandemics.

The endemic disease influenza frequently becomes epidemic and occasionally pandemic. A brief account of its incidence follows.

The dread word 'plague' means to most people some terrible event in the long distant past – the Black Death of 1347-9 or the Great Plague of 1665 – yet many men and women alive today lived through a time when the world was struck by what was probably the worst plague in recorded history, the great influenza pandemic of 1918-19. Over half the population of the world was affected; over twenty millions died of the disease or its complications.

The influenza virus was first identified in 1933 but contemporary sixteenth and seventeenth century records leave no doubt that it was already active at that time. The literature of the day shows that it was almost certainly from influenza that Mary, Queen of Scots, suffered in the Edinburgh epidemic of 1562, as the following extract from contemporary records makes clear.

Immediately upon the Queene's arrivall here she fell acquainted with a new disease that is common in this towne, called here the newe acquayntance, which passed also throughe her whole courte, neither sparinge lordes, ladyes nor damoysells, not so much as either Frenche or English. It is a plague in their heades that have yt with a great cough that remayneth with some longer, with others shorter tyme as yt findeth apte bodies for the nature of the disease. The Queene kept her bed six days. There was no appearance of danger, nor many that die of the disease except some olde folkes.

The oldest reference to influenza in England is to an epidemic in 1170: from 1500 onward the record of epidemics is well documented. Major world-wide pandemics occur irregularly; between them there are epidemics every two, three, or four years. The first important recorded pandemic was in

1781–2: it originated in Asia in the autumn of 1781 and spread all over Europe, reaching England in April 1782. It was not highly fatal: there were 200 to 300 deaths in London in June 1782 when the epidemic was at its height. The disease was predominantly one of adults – three-quarters of the adult population were affected but children were less susceptible.

Severe epidemics were recorded in 1803, 1833, and 1837, and the next great pandemic was in 1847–8. Once again the disease came from Asia, where it appeared in March 1847, and reached England in November, causing a severe winter epidemic resulting in 5,000 deaths, mostly among the elderly. From 1849–88 there were no influenza epidemics at all; then at the beginning of 1890, the next great pandemic reached England, again coming from Asia where it began in 1889. In England the disease showed four successive waves, in January 1890, May 1891, January 1892, and December 1893. The second and third waves were the most severe and caused 4,000 deaths in London alone, predominately among infants and the elderly.

Influenza was now well established in England: epidemics occurred in 1895, 1900, 1908, and the greatest pandemic of all in 1918–19. Again, in this pandemic as in the previous one, several successive waves hit England: in the summer of 1918, from October to December in the same year, and in February and March 1919. The middle wave was the most severe. Over the world as a whole the pandemic caused some twenty million deaths, over five million in India alone. Worst hit of all was Samoa where 25% of the population died. Unlike the situation in the previous pandemics the age group worst affected, and the group among whom the death rate was highest, was that of the young adults: infants and the old were still stricken, but peak incidence was in the twenty to thirty years age range.

After the great pandemic, influenza continued to occur irregularly as it did before. A severe epidemic broke out in England in 1951 which was followed by the pandemic of Asian influenza in 1957. This originated in China, reached Hong Kong, spread through Europe and North America during the summer and caused the still vividly remembered epidemic of 1957.

Since the identification of the virus in 1933, it has been possible to show that the more widespread and severe epidemics are caused by a virus known as the type A virus while the milder epidemics are due to a virus known as type B. Type A virus caused the relatively severe epidemics of 1932–3, 1936–7, and the major outbreak of 1951. The causative virus of the great 1957 pandemic was a new variant of the A type, known as the Asian virus.

Although obviously there can be no direct proof, it is probable that the 1918–19 pandemic was caused by virus of the same general type as those now known. Possibly a series of mutations produced a highly virulent variant of the A type virus against which human beings as a whole had little immunity. The excessive mutation resulting in the new form may have been brought about by exposure to mustard gas – a known mutagen in many organisms – which was used on the Western Front, where the epidemic originated in 1918. Alternatively the new variant may have been the result of 'hybridisation' between viruses of the European type and others brought to Europe by the thousands of American troops who came to France in 1918.

Three factors are primarily concerned in the birth of an epidemic: the right climatic conditions, a low level of immunity in the community, and a suitable virus. The residual immunity in a population after an epidemic precludes a further epidemic caused by the same strain of virus for some considerable time, but a mutant form may produce a second epidemic after only a few years.

Our knowledge of the history and of the erratic behaviour of the influenza virus precludes any accurate forecast of future pandemics. The course of any such outbreak could now be modified by vaccination, once the virus has been identified and the vaccine prepared; and, probably, secondary complications, the cause of many deaths in the 1918–19 pandemic, could be avoided by the use of antibiotics. Nevertheless influenza must still be regarded as a potentially serious infectious disease.

The World Health Organisation

Frequent reference has been made in the preceding pages to the work of the World Health Organisation. The chapter is concluded with a brief account of the nature and activities of this organisation.

The World Health Organisation – W.H.O. – came into

being in the summer of 1948 in the Swiss city of Geneva, already the birthplace of so many of man's hopes and aspirations. The organisation was to prove a major driving force in man's long struggle against sickness and disease, against misery and despair. The major aim of this international organisation is clearly stated in its charter – 'The attainment by all peoples of the highest possible level of health' which is to be regarded as 'one of the fundamental rights of every human being, without distinction of race, religion, political belief or economic or social condition.' Such a conception of health as a state of complete physical, mental, and social well-being and not merely the absence of disease or infirmity was an enormous advance on the idea that health is promoted merely by overcoming the agents of infection, an idea which had persisted since the sixteenth century. This does not mean that the early efforts to overcome or at least restrict the spread of infection can be disregarded: public health measures owe their very inception to the fear of contagion, of the spread of epidemics. The earliest of such steps far antedated any scientific knowledge of the cause of disease, and the concern of the authorities was neither philanthropic nor international: each nation sought only to protect itself by quarantine regulations from the major widespread infections of the day. Such quarantine measures were first adopted in Britain in 1585 but were almost totally ineffective because the ways by which diseases spread were unknown: quarantine regulations, for example, kept out the plague victim but let in the rats which had infected him. It was nearly 300 years before the concept of quarantine became less parochial: the first international conference was held in Paris in 1851, and this time the incentive was mercenary; the protection of the shipping trade with which the individual quarantine regulations of each country caused considerable interference. Many other conferences followed during the nineteenth century but lack of knowledge as well as vested trade interests detracted from their value.

The general acceptance of the germ theory of disease, as a result of the work of Louis Pasteur (1822–95), opened up a new era in the scientific understanding of infection. New discoveries followed thick and fast: before the turn of the century the bacteria which cause many of the most dreaded and prevalent diseases had been identified and described (Table 1).

Bacillus of tuberculosis	1882
Bacillus of typhoid	1884
Bacillus of diphtheria	1884
Vibrio of cholera	1884
Pneumococcus	1886
Coccus of cerebro-spinal fever	1897
Bacillus of plague	1894
Bacillus of dysentery	1898
Treponeme of syphilis	1905

TABLE 1. Dates of identification of bacteria

Effective quarantine measures, however, depend on more than knowledge of disease-causing organisms: equally important is an understanding of their methods of spread. Although the connection between the incidence of cholera and faecal-contaminated drinking water had been demonstrated in 1854, it was not until the beginning of the twentieth century that the part played by vectors in the spread of infection began to be appreciated. In the first decade of the twentieth century the role of the mosquito in the spread of malaria and yellow fever, of the flea in the spread of plague, and of the louse in the spread of typhus were all demonstrated.

During the early twentieth century information continued to accumulate rapidly and following the eleventh international congress in Paris, there was set up in 1909 the first truly international health organisation, L'Office Internationale d'Hygiene Publique, generally known as the Paris Office. Its main purpose was to collect information about methods of combating the most serious infectious diseases of the day – cholera, plague, and yellow fever. Although there was as yet no idea of a widespread war against these diseases but only a concentrated effort to prevent their spread, nevertheless the Paris Office did begin to widen its scope: to concern itself, for example, with such problems as the control of venereal disease along the major shipping lanes of the world, and with traffic in drugs. The concept of public health was beginning to take on a modern look. But the first major breakthrough did not come until after the First World War. In 1923 there was set up a new body which worked in close co-operation with the Paris Office, the Health Organisation of the League of Nations: this was the Geneva Office. The Geneva Office was the most far-seeing health organisation yet created. The realisation that many of the health problems of Europe and the New World stem from the East and that it is their prevalence there that is of major importance; the setting up of committees of experts – the technical commissions – to consider such newly appreciated health problems as housing and nutrition, and many other similar projects, marked a real breakthrough in the approach to public health. It is a sad thought that the Geneva Office, so visionary in its aims, was always handicapped by lack of funds: after undertaking to combat the post-war epidemic of typhus in Eastern Europe, after organising malaria control in South-eastern Asia, and establishing health centres in Greece and China, its funds were exhausted. It took another world war and a new international organisation to establish work on a more secure and permanent financial foundation.

The Second World War saw the virtual end of the Paris and Geneva Offices. In 1944 U.N.R.R.A. (United Nations Relief and Rehabilitation Administration) was established to help the devastated countries: this provided an effective and efficient but only temporary measure.

The Second World War left a world devastated and sick, but full of hope. The charter of the United Nations signed in San Francisco in 1945 recommended the establishment of a new international health organisation; in the summer of 1948 the World Health Assembly met in Geneva and W.H.O. was born. It absorbed into its framework U.N.R.R.A. and the Paris and Geneva Offices and when in 1949 the only other international health organisation, the Pan American Sanitary Bureau, became its American regional office, W.H.O. became in reality the health organisation of the world.

W.H.O. has a membership of nearly a hundred states. As a special agency of the United Nations, it works under the General Assembly and Economic and Social Council. In matters which are primarily concerned with the welfare of children W.H.O. works in co-operation with U.N.I.C.E.F. (United Nations International Children's Emergency Fund). W.H.O. is autonomous in matters of finance, personnel, membership, and programme of activity. Its headquarters are in Geneva, and it has a liaison office with the United Nations in New York. Its parliament, the Assembly, which meets annually at the headquarters, is directed by a non-political executive board of eighteen members from eighteen nations: six are replaced annually. It has a staff of some 1,500, the majority of whom are medical. As an independent body W.H.O. has the power to undertake any health programme so long as its budget is adequate: approximately one-twelfth of its money is contributed by the United Kingdom (Plate 4).

W.H.O. and malaria: the Thailand programme

W.H.O. is world-wide in its activities: interest in the developed countries is matched or even exceeded by its concern for the underdeveloped – the world which dies young. In no field is this more evident than in its campaign against malaria.

Since the end of the Second World War extensive malaria control campaigns have been embarked on in many malarious countries. These have been made feasible by the discovery of residual insecticides and anti-malarial drugs. W.H.O. and U.N.I.C.E.F. co-operate in many of these schemes, the former providing advice and personnel and the latter supplying insecticides, transport, and other facilities.

Two types of expert team are provided by W.H.O. – the advisory team and the malaria control demonstration team. The former team are sent to assist governments desirous of embarking upon large scale programmes, in making surveys, planning projects, and training personnel: the latter, who provide their own equipment and transport, demonstrate modern methods of control in areas of high malaria incidence and train native personnel to undertake the work themselves. In all projects undertaken malaria has been controlled and in many instances its transmission has been interrupted.

The work of an advisory team may be illustrated by reference to a project in Iran undertaken between 1950 and 1953. The team, which consisted of a malariologist, an entomologist, and a public health engineer advised the relevant government bodies on the setting up of an anti-malarial organisation, the planning and carrying out of a nation wide control programme, and the establishment of a national training programme for personnel. Throughout the whole project the W.H.O. team worked in close co-operation with their native 'opposite numbers' and as the latter become thoroughly trained they gradually took over.

Malaria control demonstrations have been carried out in many countries including Afghanistan, Burma, Cambodia, China, India, Indonesia, Iraq, Lebanon, Pakistan, Thailand,

and Vietnam: a brief description of the Thailand project will illustrate their scope and success.

Six million of the eighteen million inhabitants of Thailand live in malarious areas. The malaria control demonstration was carried out between 1949 and 1951. The team consisted of personnel provided by W.H.O. (malariologist, entomologist, sanitarian, public health nurse, and three technicians), and by the Thailand Government (malariologist, entomologist, sanitarian, laboratory technicians, nurses, and other workers); equipment, transport, and insecticides were provided by U.N.I.C.E.F.

Both demonstration and check areas were in a province in Northern Thailand. Both areas had a dense population and a high incidence of malaria. In both, irrigation of the plains for rice production had been followed by the spread of malaria from the foothills to the plains.

The first step was to identify the vector. This was found to be Aedes minimus and its incrimination was followed by an intensive investigation into its habits in order to discover on what surfaces the adults might be expected to rest so that these might be sprayed. Aedes minimus was found to be essentially an 'indoor mosquito' which prefers to rest below two metres from the floor: the results of spraying surfaces at and below this height, first in 1950 by W.H.O. personnel and again in 1951 by Thai medical officers, who had by this time assumed responsibility, were dramatic: after the first spraying the number of infants infected dropped from 29·04% to 2·59% and of the infants born after the spraying started only 0·47% were infected as against 24% in the check area. No parasites at all were found in the blood of any infants examined after the second spraying had taken place.

The effect of spraying upon the incidence of the vector species are shown in Table 2 below.

		Area I	Area II	Area III
No spraying	Aug. 1949–April 1950	9,167	5,286	No record
Area I sprayed	May 1950–Feb. 1951	—	5,888	No record
Areas I and II sprayed	May 1951–Nov. 1951	1[1]	1[1]	1,507

TABLE 2.

[1] These were young unfed specimens captured near the periphery of the area and dead before arrival at the laboratory.

The programme is now carried out entirely by the Thailand

Government and all six million people in the malarious areas are now under protection.

In any area it may become possible after a time to discontinue residual spraying either because the vector itself has been exterminated or because no more malarious patients exist in the area. Once the disease has been eradicated in this way strict precautions must be taken to ensure that it does not return. Obviously the larger the area over which eradication has been achieved the less this risk of reinfection will be.

The effectiveness of modern adulticidal residual spraying against the various species of mosquitoes means that it is no longer a mere pipe dream to envisage and plan for the eradication of malaria on a world wide scale. There is no technical reason why the disease should not be eliminated from the Americas, Europe, Australia, and parts of Asia well before the end of this century. In Africa, many Pacific Islands, and parts of South-east Asia the outlook is less hopeful.

Many obstacles still stand in the way of complete coverage of all malarious areas by residual spraying. These include poor standards of public health, indifference to, and ignorance of, the possibility of malaria eradication both on the part of those with influence and those without it, and shortage of trained personnel. Much has been achieved but much remains to be done.

The elimination of malaria from ever widening areas of the world, however, brings in its train a new series of social and economic problems. Its eradication marks the removal of one of the major checks to the growth of human populations and unless carried out concurrently with an intensive investigation into the problems of human ecology could well lead to greater human misery than the disease itself (see also Chapter VIII.).

The question of population pressure is, however, not so simple as it may appear at first sight. The present situation may perhaps be appreciated from the words of the W.H.O. publication, *Malaria, a World Problem* (1955):

> The answers to the natural query about the possible disastrous demographical effects of malaria control are: first, that no one can have the prescience necessary to justify, because of presumed future good, the present withholding from any people of those methods that are available for the cure and prevention of disease; secondly, that no one knows or can predict exactly what total population the world

can adequately support; thirdly, that there is as yet no widespread understanding of the possibilities and benefits of family planning, although in certain over-populated countries, such as India, the subject is now receiving much attention.

[Quoting Professor Hill] 'It is true that scientific research has opened up the possibility of unprecedented good, or unlimited harm, for mankind; but the use that is made of it depends in the end on the moral judgments of the whole community of men. It is totally impossible now to reverse the process of discovery: it will certainly go on. To help to guide its use aright is not a scientific dilemma, but the honourable and compelling duty of a good citizen.

'Malaria eradication is certainly not an end in itself. Malariologists, physicians, and sanitarians should, to an ever greater extent, integrate their activities into those of agriculturists, industrialists, social scientists, economists, educators, and political and religious leaders. But it has been repeatedly demonstrated that, in highly malarious countries, one of the first steps in the improvement of public welfare is the removal of malaria, which, like a blanket, stifles all aspects of human endeavour.'

CHAPTER II

The Biology of Pathogenic Organisms

The parasitisation of the body by living organisms is known as infection. The organism, which is said to be pathogenic, harms the host in which it lives; usually infection by a particular organism produces specific results, the signs and symptoms of a particular disease. Infectious diseases of man are nearly all caused by one of three types of organism, bacteria, viruses, and protozoa. There are other organisms causing human disease notably various kinds of worms and fungi; but these are very much rarer in this country and are between them responsible for not more than one tenth of one per cent of the serious illness and death caused by parasites as a whole. Of the three groups mainly responsible for disease, bacteria and protozoa have been extensively studied and knowledge of them as disease producing agents is considerable, while the viruses are the most recently discovered and still the least understood, though knowledge is increasing rapidly. There are two main reasons for this: viruses are extremely small and they can grow and multiply only within living cells; the first characteristic makes them difficult to observe, the second complicates experimental study.

Protozoan infections are rare in this country, though a great scourge in the tropics; diseases due to bacteria and viruses are of world wide incidence.

Bacteria and bacterial infections

Bacteria are morphologically simple organisms, living rod-shaped or spherical cells of microscopic size. Some are fringed all over, or at one end, with fine hair-like flagellae, others are without appendages. Each bacterium, like any other living cell, is composed of protoplasm but is unusual in that it contains no organised nucleus: the nuclear material is distributed throughout the cell instead of being aggregated. The limiting membrane of the cell is highly complicated; it usually contains

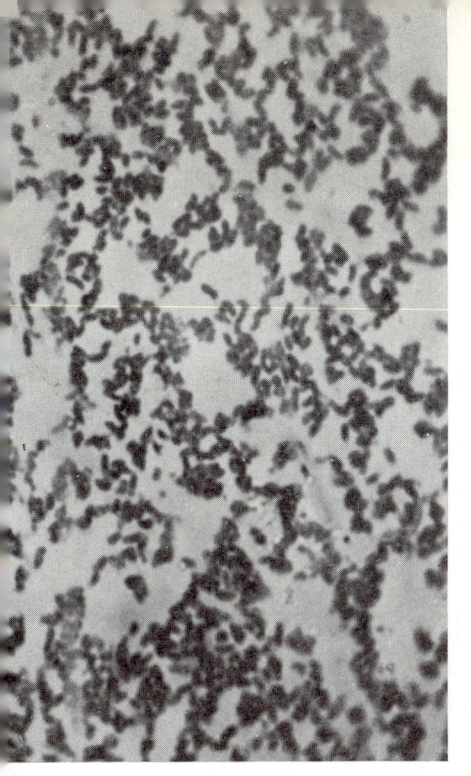 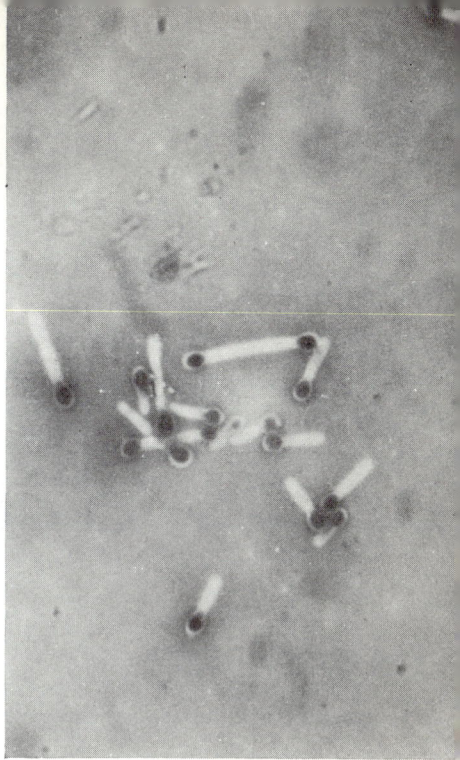

(a) Cholera bacteria ×900   (b) Tetanus bacteria ×1800

PLATE 5: Bacteria and viruses

(c) Tobacco mosaic virus ×124,00

PLATE 6: The pioneer and the outcome of his work

(a) Louis Pasteur 1822–1895

(b) The modern milk pasteurising plant which immortalises his name

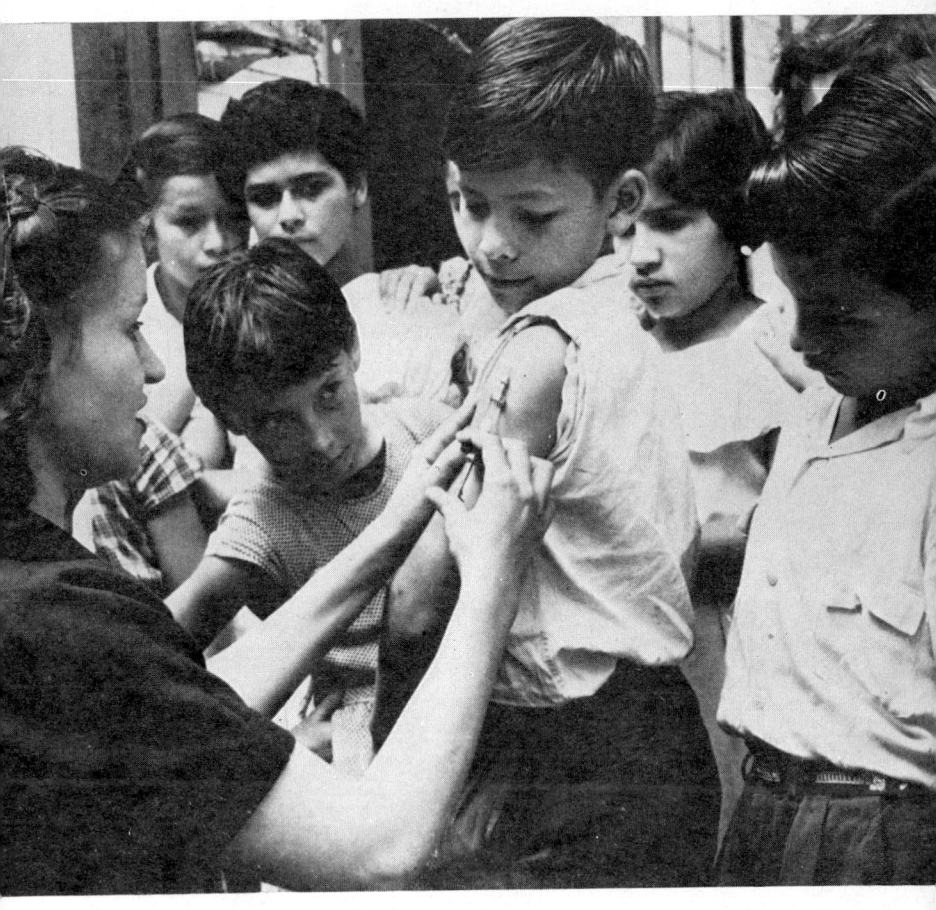

PLATE 7: Costa Rican school children are protected from tuberculosis by BCG injections

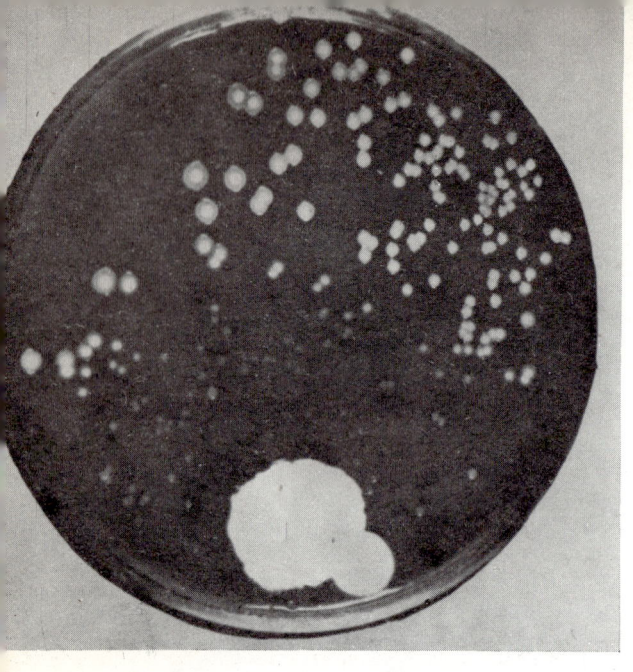

(a) The historic plate—the mould is inhibiting the growth of bacteria

PLATE 8: Penicillin—miracle drug

(b) Where it all began—Flemming's laboratory at St Mary's Hospital

complex polysaccharides which may form a thick sticky layer round the bacterium.

Bacteria reproduce by division; after elongation the substance is nipped into two. Given favourable conditions so that no limiting factors operate, bacteria will divide every twenty minutes; at this rate a single bacterium will become over a million in twenty four hours. A modified type of sexual reproduction has recently been described in a limited number of bacteria but this has not been observed in any of the disease producing types. Some bacteria are able to produce spores to tide them over a period in an environment unsuitable for growth; a hard shell develops round the contents of the bacterium and within this it can survive for years.

Bacteria occur everywhere, in soil, air, and water but are particularly abundant in any type of dead organic matter, and their activity exerts a profound influence upon all other forms of life, plant and animal, including man. In their relationship to man bacteria fall into three groups; those which are potentially dangerous to him, those to which he is indifferent, and those without which the very continuation of his life would be impossible. It is with this first group that we are concerned in the present context.

The bacterium is built up of the same basic substances as any other living organism: proteins constructed from the same range of amino acids, the same type of nucleic acids, the same fats, phospholipids and sterols, and the same vitamins incorporated in the enzyme systems. Like any other living organism, too, the bacterium constantly expends energy. All these complex substances in its protoplasm have to be built up out of, and the necessary energy obtained from, the material which the bacterium absorbs from its environment.

The simplest bacteria have very modest requirements; under experimental conditions they will grow and thrive provided that the simple salts and glucose necessary for self-construction and energy are available. Others are, however, much more demanding in their requirements; several of the amino acids and vitamins which they require must be provided already elaborated. The pathogenic or disease-producing forms all belong to this more exacting group. The pathogenic bacteria are probably all descended from free living forms which, having lost some of their own synthesising ability, have survived only by becoming saprophytes or parasites, often of a highly specialised type. These bacteria, which live on dead or living organic material, must first break this down into simple substances which can be absorbed by and assimilated into the substance of the bacteria themselves. This is possible because all bacteria contain a very large number of enzyme systems some of which, though not all, are contained in the surface layers. It is these surfaces which affect the surrounding medium and make its compounds suitable for bacterial use. The surfaces are always the site of intense chemical activity; it is not surprising therefore that the presence of bacteria within living body tissues has such a disrupting effect upon their metabolism.

Dead organic matter is an excellent medium for the growth of bacteria and they are found abundantly in the dead material both on the surface of and within the human body. The outermost cells of the skin are dead and large numbers of bacteria make their home there and also in the lining of the mouth, nose, and throat. Large numbers also live in the food remains in the large intestine where they form about half the bulk of the faeces. As long as these bacteria live on dead matter they are quite harmless, but they are in an excellent situation for entry into the living tissues and this is probably how the pathogenic forms have evolved. The skin, the membrane lining the exits from and entrances into the body, and the alimentary canal, are the four main routes through which bacteria enter the body. Furthermore, many disease-producing bacteria are closely related to or even identical with forms living harmlessly in other situations, and the region where they make their first entry is nearly always the usual home of the non-pathogenic forms.

On the surface of the skin one type of bacterium, the staphylococcus, is predominant. Common skin infections, pimples and boils, are nearly always due to invasion of the living tissues by closely related staphylococcal types. These pathogenic forms have further developed the power of living in tissues other than the skin; if they invade the blood they cause staphylococcal septicaemia, or blood poisoning, while the acute bone disease, osteomyelitis, is also a staphylococcal infection.

Various types of bacteria are common on the mucous membrane of the mouth, throat, and tonsils; harmless streptococci, pneumococci, and meningococci may all be present. Closely related pathogenic streptococci cause tonsillitis and scarlet fever, while pathogenic pneumococci and meningococci cause pneumonia and meningitis. Commonly, too, the throat harbours harmless rod-like bacilli; a closely related form is responsible for diphtheria.

In the intestine, the predominant bacteria are rod-like bacilli, dozens of varieties of which have been identified. From these harmless types have evolved the dangerous typhoid and dysentery bacilli.

These are but a few examples; members of many of the groups of bacteria have become parasitic; some cause disease and others are tolerated. Most human beings have established a balanced relationship with a large number of parasitic forms; only if the pathogenic bacteria reach a susceptible host or if the resistance of the host is lowered, are disease symptoms produced.

How bacteria harm the body

Pathogenic bacteria have two weapons of attack in the human body: they may themselves invade and destroy the tissues or they may produce toxins which do the harm. Invasive bacteria multiply at the site of infection and then spread, either by growing through the tissues or by being carried in the blood or lymph. These bacteria produce a variety of chemical substances whose action weakens the defences of the host, and by breaking these defences down they make invasion easier. These substances include haemolysins which break down red blood cells, leucocidins which destroy leucocytes, fibrinolysins which dissolve blood clots and so facilitate bacterial spread, and finally the substance hyaluronidase. Hyaluronidase is an enzyme which hydrolyses hyaluronic acid, the complex polysaccharide which is a constituent of normal animal tissues and is responsible for their viscosity. It is this viscosity which helps to prevent the spread of invading bacteria. If it is reduced by the hydrolysising effect on hyaluronic acid of the hyaluronidase produced by the invading bacteria, rapid spread of the bacteria is facilitated. For this reason hyaluronidase is often called the spreading factor.

Toxins operate not against the defences of the body but against the tissues themselves, either destroying them or impairing their function; their action does not necessarily increase the pathogen's power of survival.

Toxins are usually described as being of two types, exotoxins and endotoxins, though it is now realised that the distinction between them is not so clear cut as it was originally thought to be. Exotoxins, the most powerful poisons known, far more poisonous than snake venom or strychnine, are active in very small doses. They are proteins which diffuse through the membrane of the living bacterium which produced them, into the susceptible tissue where they act as enzymes, destroying some essential part of the cells or preventing some vital metabolic process. Different exotoxins show marked affinities for different types of tissues. Diseases due to bacteria which produce exotoxins include diphtheria, tetanus, botulism, and scarlet fever: in the first three the toxins affect the cells of the central nervous system, in the fourth, those of the skin. Endotoxins are poisonous intrabacterial substances; they do not diffuse into the surrounding medium and are liberated only when the bacterium is destroyed. They are very much less potent than exotoxins, show no definite tissue affinities, and are only slightly antigenic.[1] Some toxins show some of the properties of both types; it is not yet always possible to state with certainty to which class the toxin produced by a particular bacterium belongs.

Bacterial diseases of man

Some bacteria possess only one of the two possible weapons of attack, others have both. Anthrax, a disease of cattle, pigs, and sheep is caused by an invasive bacterium which produces no toxins. Anthrax spores, lodged in wool or hides, may enter human tissues through abrasions in the skin. Within the skin the spores germinate and the bacteria multiply rapidly. The surrounding tissues are destroyed and filled with bacteria; the dead tissues liberate poisons which help in the destruction of living cells. Eventually blood vessels are involved in the destruction and the bacteria are distributed by the blood to all parts of the body. Capillaries, plugged by bacteria, burst and the bacteria liberated into the tissues grow and multiply. Death results when the activity of a vital organ is interfered with.

The most dangerous bacteria of all are naturally those which produce exotoxins. This capacity is, in different types, combined with different degrees of invasiveness. The diphtheria

---

[1]. See page 95.

bacillus has no invasive power: the responsible bacterium never penetrates beyond the nose and throat. Diphtheria, which was once one of the major killing diseases of children in this country, is now uncommon: this dramatic decrease in its incidence is due to immunisation (see page 87). Today no child in this country need die of this once dread disease. The responsible organism, Corynebacterium diphtheriae, exists in three forms, causing diseases of varying severity. In a severe clinical case the presence of the bacteria in the throat results in the development of a yellowish-white membrane on the tonsils and possibly, too, on the surrounding tissues: this membrane may block the trachea and immediate surgery is then needed to save the child's life. But an equally grave danger comes from the exotoxin which the bacteria produce. This toxin is absorbed into the blood and by its effect on the central nervous system may cause paralysis of palate, eye muscles, heart, pharyngeal, laryngeal, and respiratory muscles. Expert nursing is necessary to bring the patient through this series of hazards. But today no such case need ever be seen: even if the child has not previously been immunised, early treatment with antitoxic serum completely modifies the course of the disease (see page 87).

The Clostridia, a group of bacteria which produce most powerful exotoxins, vary in their capacity to invade. A particularly interesting species is C. botulinum, an organism which is occasionally found in spoiled, often tinned, foodstuffs. If the food is eaten the absorption of the toxin may cause death from botulism even if the toxin only, and no actual bacteria, enters the body. It is indeed doubtful if the bacteria have any power at all to invade the alimentary canal. The members of another species, C. tetani, live harmlessly in the gut of many grazing animals and are frequently present in the soil. These bacteria may get into the body in deep, soil-contaminated wounds such as those caused by the spike of a running shoe, the prong of a garden fork, or a long sharp thorn. These bacteria invade only to a very limited extent but they may produce sufficient exotoxin to cause the characteristic symptoms of the disease tetanus or lockjaw. The toxin has a particular affinity for the anterior horn cells of the spinal cord which it reaches by way of the axons which terminate in the damaged area. The result is violent tonic contraction of the muscles innervated by the affected nerve cells. In wounds infected with the species C. welchii, on the other hand, the tissues destroyed by the toxins and by the gas produced by the bacteria, are rapidly invaded by the bacteria and the condition of gas gangrene develops (Plate 5).

Streptococci are spherical bacteria which are arranged in chains of varying lengths. There are a very large number of species one of which, Streptococcus haemolyticus, is highly pathogenic to man. Some strains of this species have considerable invasive powers, some produce a wide range of toxic substances in addition to a potent exotoxin. Various diseases are caused by Streptococcus haemolyticus; their clinical manifestations depend upon the site of entry of the bacteria into the body, upon whether or not, and to what extent, they invade the tissues, upon the virulence and quantity of toxin produced and upon the resistance of the infected individual. If, for example, the bacteria enter the body by way of the mucous membrane of the respiratory tract, a common site of infection, they usually remain in the throat: if the effect is largely local, tonsillitis develops, but if the toxins spread via the blood stream to the skin, the characteristic rash of scarlet fever appears. Whether the patient develops tonsillitis or scarlet fever appears to depend partly on his resistance and partly on the toxigenicity of the infecting strain. From the throat the streptococci may also reach the middle ear and cause otitis media, or even the brain itself resulting in meningitis. The streptococci are also often identified in the throats of patients with acute rheumatic fever. Introduced into the subcutaneous tissue when the skin is injured, the streptococci may cause a local septic condition or they may spread through the body to cause general blood poisoning or streptococcal septicaemia. If introduced into the disorganised tissues of the uterus after childbirth by the mother herself, or by an attendant, the bacteria rapidly invade the tissues and produce a potent exotoxin: the result is puerperal fever.

Fortunately for man a large number of pathogenic bacteria produce not exo- but endotoxins: the majority of these bacteria, however, have considerable invasive powers. A marked exception is the bacterium, Vibrio cholerae, which causes cholera in man. The way the organism, which is present in the faeces of patients and carriers, is spread by contaminated drinking water, has already been described. The organisms themselves remain in the intestine; only very rarely do they invade the blood. The characteristic symptoms, fever, abdominal pain, and diarrhoea are due to absorbed endotoxin (Plate 5).

Whooping cough, a common and serious disease of children, is caused by a bacterium Haemophillus pertussis, which invades only the tissues of the upper respiratory tract into which it is introduced by droplet infection. Between them, the organisms themselves and the mucus which they produce clog and destroy the cilia of the tract: the debris is only expelled by the spasms of coughing characteristic of the disease. The long-drawn inspiration which follows such a paroxysm causes the characteristic whoop; this may be followed by vomiting. The endotoxins absorbed into the blood may affect the central nervous system. The course of the disease is very prolonged and its effects debilitating: a severe attack may interfere very considerably with the growth of a young patient.

Bacillary dysentery, an acute and painful disease, is caused by the Shigella group of bacteria which enter the alimentary canal in contaminated food and water. The organisms remain in the large intestine but the endotoxins are absorbed into the blood. In one type, S. shigae, an exotoxin may be produced and cause on absorption severe nervous symptoms.

Bacteria of the Salmonella genus also introduced into the body in food and water are the cause of enteric fevers and of bacterial food infections. These bacteria have very considerable invasive powers and the destruction of tissue entailed is responsible for the severe symptoms which develop. The enteric fevers, typhoid and paratyphoid, are caused by Salmonella typhi and Salmonella paratyphi respectively: the two diseases are similar in many ways but the former is usually much more severe. The bacteria reach the spleen, liver, and mesenteric glands from the intestine via the lymphatics and in these organs they proliferate rapidly, often entering the gall bladder. After some fourteen days they enter the blood and the characteristic symptoms then appear. At this stage the bacteria cause considerable disintegration of the intestinal wall: this is responsible for many of the most serious symptoms.

Other species of Salmonella with variable invasive powers cause bacterial food infections ranging from mild to very severe. The disease is an acute illness of short duration, the onset of the disease coming some eight to forty-eight hours after eating food in which the causal bacteria are multiplying. The foods include meat, fish, milk, dairy produce, drinking water, and occasionally eggs laid by infected ducks.

Many species of staphylococci, spherical bacteria which occur in grape-like clusters, live harmlessly on human skin and in many healthy throats. If entry to underlying tissues is gained, either through minute abrasions, by way of a hair follicle, or through the mucous membrane of the throat, local skin infections, pimples or boils or a septic sore throat, may follow. Usually the bacteria show little power of invasion: general infection of the blood may, however, occur, causing staphylococcal septicaemia. Infection of wounds by penicillin-resistant strains of staphylococci is a serious problem in hospitals.

One great danger of pathogenic staphylococci follows their transfer to food, either from infected skin during handling or from infected throats during coughing. In foods such as cooked meats and cream, the staphylococci thrive and give rise to endotoxins. If this food is eaten by man, although the bacteria are themselves unable to invade the tissues of the alimentary canal, the toxins may be absorbed and cause acute gastro-intestinal distress. The symptoms appear within two to four hours of eating the toxic food and the patient suffers an attack of food poisoning. The severity of the condition varies, but the sickness is less severe than botulism, and those who absorb staphylococci toxins, though often violently ill, usually recover.

The gonococcus, a bacterium which causes gonorrhoea and which cannot survive for long outside the human body, is spread by sexual intercourse. It thrives in the reproductive tract where it causes severe inflammation. It may spread over the whole body causing a general infection, joints and heart being especially affected. A harmful exotoxin is also produced.

Bubonic plague, already described in Chapter I, is caused by a bacillus, Pasteurella pestis, with great invasive powers, which also produces a powerful endotoxin. Tuberculosis, the 'white plague' is due to the bacillus Myobacterium tuberculosis. This bacillus exists in a number of strains of which two, the human and the bovine, affect man. The tubercle bacillus is unique in many ways: though possessed of considerable invasive powers it usually spreads only slowly and the disease can be of very long duration. Infection is usually by way of the respiratory tract or the alimentary canal; the human strain usually enters by the former route, the bovine by the latter. The respiratory type is spread by droplet infection or from dried sputum; the bovine strain is introduced into the body in milk from infected cows.

The slow acting tubercle bacilli on entering the body usually provoke no inflammatory reaction but quickly settle down in the tissues and are walled off by leucocytes. In this way are formed the tiny nodules or tubercles which give the disease its name. The subsequent history of these first formed tubercles depends upon a number of factors which include the age and power of resistance of the subject and the site of entry: genetic factors, too, may play some part.

The bacillus Myobacterium leprae, closely related to M. tuberculosis, is the cause of leprosy. The bacterium may affect the peripheral nerves or the skin, giving rise to two distinct forms of the disease, the neural and the cutaneous. In the former, the characteristic symptom is total loss of sensation in the affected parts; the latter is typified by the development of nodules on the face, arms, legs, and trunk, which produce gross deformity. The incubation period of both forms of the disease is very variable, possibly as short as a few months but often as long as twenty-five years. The average time is probably between two and seven years.

Leprosy may be transmitted by direct contact but it has a very low order of communicability. Under modern conditions it is acquired only after long, close association with an affected individual. Conditions which favour its spread are poor personal hygiene and a low standard of living, especially in areas with a hot, humid climate. At present the disease is confined to parts of Japan, China, North India, and South America, and to a few areas in Texas and Louisiana. There are probably between one and two million cases in the world today.

Treponemes and Treponematosis

The Treponemes are a group of thread-like, spirally-coiled bacteria with tapering ends which often bear flagella. The different species of Treponemes have been identified as the causative agents of a number of different infections in man, collectively known as the treponematoses.

Treponema pallidum causes sporadic or venereal, and endemic or non-venereal syphilis, both of which have a wide

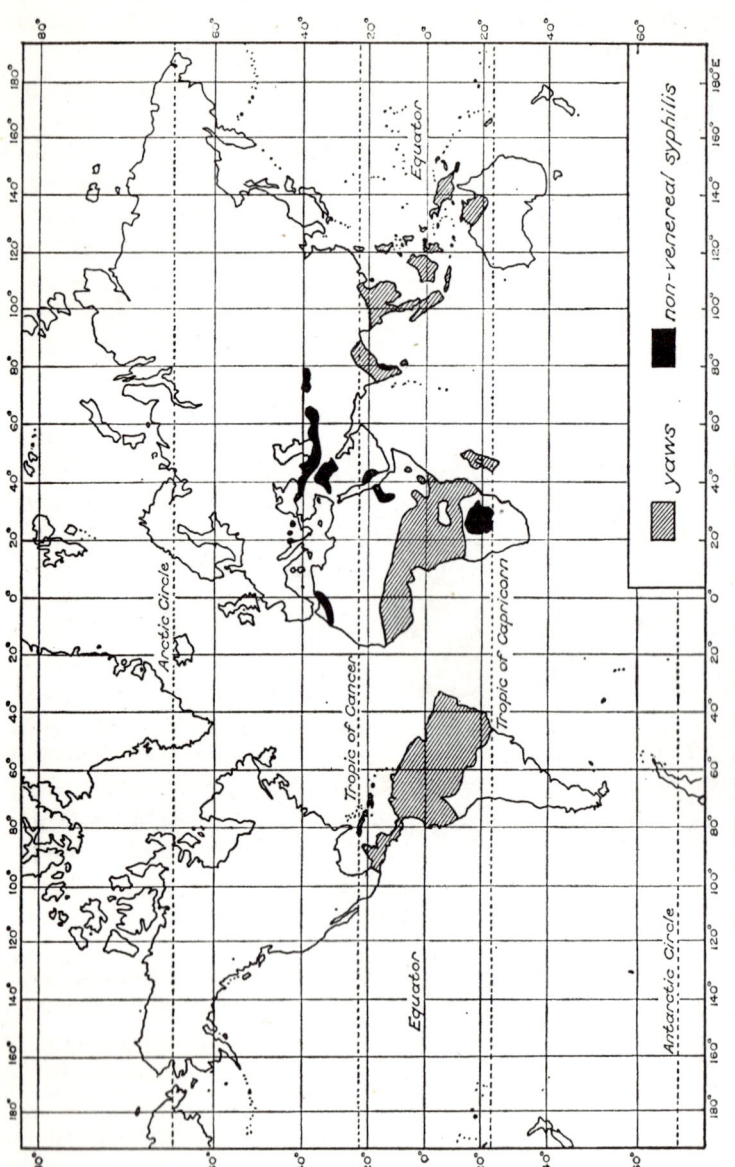

FIG. 6. World distribution of non-venereal Treponematoses.

distribution throughout the world, and a number of more local diseases. Treponema pertenue causes yaws. With the exception of sporadic syphilis which is spread venereally, other treponematoses are spread by direct contact or by indirect transfer. The geographical distribution of the various treponematoses is shown in Figure 6.

Treponema pallidum is a delicate, flagellated organism between six and fourteen microns in length. There are usually between six and twelve coils in its spiral body. The organism is an obligate parasite which does not thrive away from its host: this, coupled with its extreme sensitivity to drying out, to weak disinfectants and even to soap and water, means that it is rarely spread except by direct transmission. The only natural host is man.

It is estimated that there are at least twenty million cases of sporadic syphilis distributed throughout the world, the major incidence being among young adults. After penetrating the skin, usually of the genitalia, occasionally of the lips, mouth or fingers, the treponemes multiply and invade the tissues to produce a small painless ulcer or chancre at the site of entry. This sore, which marks the primary stage of the disease, usually heals in four to six weeks and may pass quite unnoticed. The treponemes, however, continue to multiply, invade the tissues and are distributed round the body in the blood. After a few weeks, or even as long as a year, without symptoms, the secondary stage of the disease develops: the patient has a fever accompanied by joint pains, enlarged lymph nodes and many small ulcer-like sores on the skin and mucous membrane of the mouth and throat. These sores contain innumerable treponemes and are highly infectious. The secondary stage usually fades in a short time but the organisms continue to invade the tissues and later, often in a few months, more usually after four to six years, sometimes after as long as thirty years, the tertiary stage of the disease becomes evident. By now the organisms have invaded the central nervous system, the liver, the spleen, and the heart and blood vessels: heart failure, locomotor disturbances, paralysis, insanity, and blindness may result.

Treponema pallidum from the blood of a syphilitic woman may pass through the placenta and invade the foetus to give rise to a tragic form of the disease, congenital syphilis. Early infection may result in the death of the foetus; a child who survives may be born with, or develop in the first few weeks of life, clinical symptoms of secondary syphilis. In other instances, the child may be apparently normal at birth, but may develop at any time during the first twenty years of life, the symptoms of tertiary syphilis – changes in the teeth and skeleton, severe eye troubles and deafness. Congenital syphilis can be prevented by early and adequate treatment of the pregnant woman (see Chapter III).

Endemic syphilis is transmitted directly, or indirectly by common household utensils, among children and young adolescents living under primitive, over-crowded conditions. The characteristic sign of the disease is the development of extensive mucous patches around the mouth. These skin lesions are essentially similar to those of venereally acquired syphilis, and, as in the latter, skeletal, cardio-vascular, and nervous systems become involved. Endemic syphilis is, however, essentially a disease of childhood and early adolescence while the peak incidence of the venereal disease is among young adults.

Yaws is essentially a disease of childhood prevalent in, and almost confined to, the regions between the tropics of Cancer and Capricorn, and there are probably some fifty million cases in these areas. The treponeme enters through an abrasion, usually on exposed parts of the body, and the infection results in the development of a primary sore, followed by lesions in the bones and joints. The disease persists, with intermissions and relapses, for many years and extensive tissue destruction leads in time to permanent invalidism and inability to work.

Viruses and virus infections

To be introduced to the viruses is to become acquainted for the first time with the members of a unique and almost incredible group of living things – the denizens of the world of the infinitely small. But their incredible minuteness is not their only unique feature; indeed when we come to study the viruses we have to revise our very conception of what constitutes a living creature at all, for here we deal not with a living cell but with a living aggregate of molecules. For the virus is not a living unit in the long familiar sense of the word but a number of chemical molecules arranged in a specific pattern and having the property of self-reproduction – the essential criterion of life itself.

The virus differs from the bacterium in at least one other important characteristic: while the bacterium, provided it is supplied with certain essential raw materials, is capable of independent existence, the virus can live and reproduce only within a living cell. Cells of many different types act as hosts: plant, animal, and those of the bacteria themselves, and each virus has its own specific type of cell to which it is confined: the tobacco mosaic virus, for example, will live only in the cells of the tobacco plant; the influenza virus only in those of the upper respiratory tract.

Only a very few viruses can even be seen with the ordinary light microscope because the visible light rays used to provide illumination in such an instrument are too long to resolve the details of any particle of dimensions less than 250 millimicrons (mμ),[1] and only a few of the largest viruses reach such a size. But the invention in 1938 of the electron microscope, in which a stream of electrons replaces the visible light rays, made it possible for the first time to investigate microscopically the nature of a far wider range of viruses, including many of the smallest. When such a study became possible scientists were amazed to find that the boundary set by the wave length of visible light coincides roughly with that between two completely different forms of life.

In the world of viruses as in that of the more familiar living organisms there is considerable variety both in shape and in size. The animal viruses – those which infect animal cells – which have so far been described are spherical or polyhedral; plant viruses appear to be rod-shaped, and the bacteriophages – those which invade bacteria – are tadpole-shaped with a head and either a very short or a longer tail. The differences in size are relatively as great as those between an elephant and a mouse: the largest viruses described, those which cause psittacosis (parrot disease) and smallpox, have diameters of 275 and 200 millimicrons respectively; the virus causing herpes simplex (cold sores) is 50 millimicrons in diameter; the two smallest so far identified and described, those causing foot and mouth disease and poliomyelitis, measure 15 and 20 millimicrons across respectively.

Although the electron microscope took the study of viruses much further, it was soon evident that it was a tool which was

1. m$\mu = \frac{1}{1000}\mu$; $\mu = \frac{1}{1000}$mm.

not going to prise from them all their secrets: further techniques still had to be developed. Recent experimental work has made it possible to break down some viruses into their component parts and so to investigate their chemical nature. It has also been possible to prepare some viruses in crystalline form and investigate their structure by the X-ray techniques which have been used so successfully in the study of a wide range of crystals.

Such studies have revealed that many viruses consist chemically of only two types of substance – proteins and nucleic acids (though some of the larger ones also contain lipids). In the plant viruses the nucleic acid appears to be RNA; in the animal, DNA or RNA; and in the bacterial viruses DNA only. The first virus to be studied in detail was the tobacco mosaic virus. This virus is a rod-shaped particle up to 300 millimicrons in length and 15 millimicrons in diameter. It is 94·4% protein and 5·6% nucleic acid, a lower proportion of nucleic acid than in viruses studied later. The nucleic acid forms a core in the centre of the virus and the protein is arranged round it. Each protein sub-unit is a single peptide chain of about 145 amino acids and the units all have a similar, though not necessarily identical, structure. The whole virus has a spiral form; there are a large number of individual protein sub-units, probably about 2,800, which have the form of triangular slabs, fitting round the core of nucleic acid like the steps of a spiral staircase. There are 49 sub-units on three tiers of the spiral or helix. The RNA appears to be in the form of a single strand which follows the twists of the helix (Plate 5).

The poliomyelitis virus consists of 60 similar protein units arranged like the drupes of a blackberry round a central core of RNA. The whole mass, the core of RNA with its 60 surrounding sub-units of protein, is polyhedral in shape with the symmetry of an icosahedron (a closed shape with twenty plane faces). Other spherical viruses studied also appear to have icosahedral symmetry; the number of protein sub-units varies:

Adenovirus from the human throat	252 protein sub-units
Tomato bushy stunt	92 protein sub-units
Virus from Red Spider	42 protein sub-units
Turnip yellow mosaic	32 protein sub-units
Bacteriophage X174	12 protein sub-units

The bacteriophage T_2, a large virus which invades and destroys the bacterium, Bacillus coli, which lives in the large intestine, has a hexagonal head and a long hollow tail: again the remarkable symmetry of the head may be conferred upon it by the nucleic acid, this time DNA, which the protein shell surrounds.

Virus-containing material can be obtained from the susceptible cells of an infected individual; for experimental study and later for the preparation of vaccines, a suitable alternative host must be found in the tissues of which the particular virus can grow and reproduce and give evidence of its activity. This experimental work is complicated by the fact that some viruses are highly selective as to the cells in which they will grow in the body; for example, the poliomyelitis virus grows in the cells of the spinal cord. In many cases, including poliomyelitis, alternative laboratory hosts have only recently been found. Other viruses are less specific: generally, the less active the virus is in producing disease the wider its range of host cells. In the laboratory viruses are most often grown in one of three types of living cells: those of the white mouse, of the chick embryo, and those of tissue cultures. The white mouse will serve as host to a wide range of viruses, provided the viruses are introduced directly into the susceptible tissues instead of just leaving the animal to 'catch' the disease: much of the research work on influenza has been carried out in this way. The tissues of growing chick embryos, protected by the shell and fibrous skin, are sterile and the cells of the embryonic membranes are highly susceptible to a wide range of virus diseases. Inoculation of the virus into the egg in such a way that it reaches the cells of the most susceptible membrane is followed by a severe infection providing a rich supply of the virus. Influenza, yellow fever virus, and typhus rickettsia (see page 62) can be grown in this way. Finally, some viruses can be grown in the cells of tissue cultures. A tissue culture consists of living cells, usually embryonic, kept alive outside the parent body. In the cells of the tissue any virus to which they are susceptible can be successfully grown. In one of these ways supplies of a large number of viruses can now be obtained for experimental study and for the preparation and testing of vaccines.

The aspect of viruses which is of prime importance to man is naturally that which concerns their relationship to his tissues: how they enter into and reproduce within his cells and how they destroy his living tissues. Increased knowledge of virus structure gives greater understanding of these problems. Experimental work has shown, for example, that it is the core of the virus, the nucleic acid, which transmits the infection: the protein shell acts as a form of packaging which protects the nucleic acid from those substances present in the host cells which might destroy it. The presence of such substances in the cells has been successfully demonstrated. But before it can reproduce itself the virus must shed its sheath. This appears to take place either outside the host cell, only the nucleic acid actually entering the cell at all, or in some place inside the cell where the virus is temporarily at least in comparative safety. The nucleic acid then reproduces itself and each new unit fabricates a new protein sheath for itself from the substance of the host cell. The process is presumably controlled by the nucleic acid; one cannot but recall the essentially similar role of the DNA of the genes, and of the RNA of the cytoplasm in normal protein metabolism (see Vol. I).

The process of virus entry has been studied in detail in the bacteriophage T_2. When the virus comes into contact, the tip of its tail dissolves the bacterial wall, the DNA from the head is shot into the bacterium via the tail leaving the protein sheath behind: the whole virus, in fact, acts like a hypodermic syringe. Within seven minutes of its entry the DNA has begun to multiply; in ten, there are fifty separate particles. Each of these now synthesises a new protein sheath around itself and twenty minutes after the first invasion the bacterium bursts and the fifty new viruses are shed into the medium, ready to enter fresh bacteria.

A virus which has been investigated very thoroughly is that which causes influenza in man. Under normal conditions this virus attaches itself to the cells lining the bronchioles and so causes influenza; experimentally it will affect the cells of the allantois of a chick embryo and from this source most of the information concerning its behaviour has been obtained. The surfaces of the cells of the bronchioles – and of the allantois – like all other cell surfaces, are very elaborate; they contain amongst other substances a number of highly complex carbohydrates. Many of these carbohydrates consist of elongated molecules forming a network over the surface of the cell. Certain points on this mesh, the carbohydrate receptors, correspond with certain points on the virus in exactly the same way as enzyme molecules correspond with those of the substrate (see Vol. I). When these two points – the carbohydrate receptors and the relevant protein molecules of the virus surface – come into contact, they unite. The nucleic acid of the virus then enters the cell and behaves in the same way as the bacteriophage.

Further experimental work has shown that the mumps virus enters the cell in the same way as the influenza virus; others, like but not identical with, the poliomyelitis virus, enter in a somewhat similar way. Probably others, like T_2, enter more directly. In infected human tissue the virus continues to spread from cell to cell until all susceptible tissue is involved, or until the progress of the virus is checked by some other means.

Recently extensive study has been made of the virus infection of the eyes, trachoma. The causative agent of trachoma has now been identified as a large virus of the same group as that which causes psittacosis. The virus consists of a central core of DNA surrounded by a protein coat. As it enters a susceptible cell of the conjunctiva the virus sheds its protein coat and the naked DNA, after entry, becomes for a while unidentifiable, during which time it presumably acts as a template for the formation of RNA particles; these appear some three hours after infection, aggregated together as the inclusion body, lying in a vacuole near the nucleus of the infected cell. The inclusion body grows until it has engulfed practically all the cytoplasm and fills the cell. Within it, some twenty-two hours after infection, large numbers of DNA particles appear. Each DNA particle then develops a protein jacket to become a new virus and some seventy hours after the initial infection the cell bursts and the new viruses escape to infect neighbouring cells (Fig. 7).

As soon as a virus invades a living cell it diverts the machinery of this cell to its own purposes. The nucleic acid of the virus begins to dominate the metabolism of the cell in order to manufacture the protein and nucleic acid necessary for its reproduction. The normal metabolism of the cell breaks down completely: it is the effects of this which manifest themselves as disease.

The virus causing an infectious disease, then, enters the susceptible cell and multiplies within it, soon spreading the infection to other cells within the body. The spread may be limited to cells of the same type as those originally infected or it

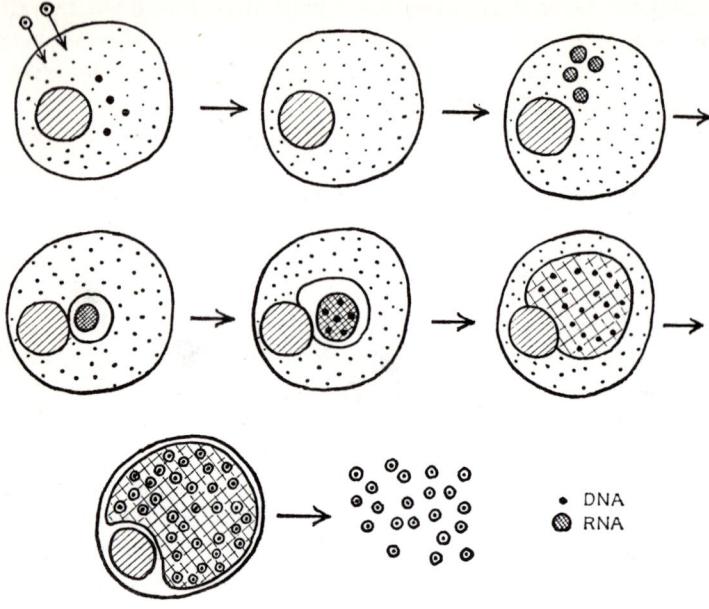

Top row left — *virus enters cell and sheds Protein coat*
         centre — *no virus visible*
         right — *RNA particles appear*
Centre row left — *RNA particles form inclusion body in vacuole*
         centre — *new DNA particles appear in inclusion body*
         right — *amount of DNA increases and inclusion body grows*
Bottom row left — *inclusion body fills cell – DNA particles develop protein jackets*
         right — *new virus particles escape from cell*

FIG. 7. The invasion of the cell by the Trachoma virus.

may spread more widely infecting cells of a variety of types. This difference in behaviour produces two distinct patterns in the history of virus diseases. The characteristic symptoms of the disease may follow quickly after the initial infection, as in influenza, or they may appear only after an interval of days or even weeks as in measles. The first pattern, with short incubation, is typical of those diseases where cells of one type only are susceptible. In influenza, the virus, as already described, enters the cells of the bronchioles and reproduces within them. The new viruses are liberated from the destroyed cells onto the surface of the lining membrane where they enter and infect more and more surface cells. A new generation is liberated every five to eight hours; after three or four generations have been produced every susceptible cell is infected and the attack is at its height – some fifteen to thirty hours after the original infection. Some viruses may enter the blood or lymph but they find no susceptible host cells to enter.

The second pattern, with long incubation, is characteristic of diseases due to viruses which can thrive in cells of more than one type. In measles, for example, the virus enters the cells of the respiratory membrane where it multiplies. It then enters the lymph and blood and so reaches all parts of the body. In the skin it finds other susceptible cells and its presence in these, two or three weeks after the original infection, produces the characteristic measles rash.

Every virus disease, whether of long- or short-term incubation, has certain signs and symptoms. Some of these, for instance, the spots of chickenpox or the paralysis of poliomyelitis, are peculiar to the specific disease; many diseases are accompanied by others, such as a high temperature, headache, and shivering. Some symptoms, like post-poliomyelitis paralysis, are due to loss of normal function of the affected cells following their destruction by the virus, others are the effects of the products of cell disintegration. The activity of the virus completely disrupts cell metabolism and the damaged cell releases substances which cause both local and general symptoms. In some cases the damaged cells release substances which stimulate neighbouring cells to abnormal activity. Infected skin cells usually grow and multiply rapidly producing the nodule-like pocks characteristic of many virus diseases in which skin tissue is involved. As the infected cells die and disintegrate a fluid filled blister is formed in the centre of each pock. The products of cell disintegration also enter the blood and lymph and spread throughout the body. The feverish symptoms, high temperatures, shivering, and headache accompanying many virus infections, are thought to be due to the poisonous effects of these substances. There is no evidence that viruses themselves produce toxins.

One of the most serious virus infections is poliomyelitis (infantile paralysis). Three different strains of the virus, Lansing, Leon, and Brunhilde are able to cause the disease; they probably enter by the mouth and invade the gastro-intestinal tract. From here they enter the blood and if the disease follows its full course they pass to the central nervous system. Here they attack particularly the anterior horn cells, no motor impulses reach the muscles innervated by the affected anterior horn cells and a flaccid paralysis of the muscles follows. In some instances the cells are completely destroyed and the paralysis is then permanent, in others they are temporarily poisoned and considerable, often rapid, recovery from paralysis follows.

During the acute stage of the disease, the virus is present in the saliva and in the faeces. Many people who are infected develop a mild illness only; a general feeling of malaise often with an apparent cold and headache. These symptoms are due to the presence of the virus in the blood. Later in a small percentage of those infected the more severe symptoms of the major disease appear, accompanied by varying degrees of temporary or permanent paralysis. Most recovery from paralysis takes place during the first few weeks after its onset, though there may be gradual recovery for as long as six months. When respiratory muscles are involved the patient has to be nursed in an iron lung or be provided with some other device to aid respiration.

A well known disease of both children and adults is jaundice. The name jaundice literally means yellowness, and the disease is so named because of the characteristic yellow colour which the patient shows. This yellowness is caused by an accumulation of bile pigments in the blood. The commonest form of jaundice, especially in children, is infective hepatitis, a type in which the symptoms are due to inflammation of the liver caused by a virus infection. The disease is probably spread by droplet and faecal infection. The patient suffers from headache, nausea and vomiting, followed by the characteristic yellowing, seen first in the eyes.

An extremely serious disease, especially of very young children, is acute gastro-enteritis. This disease which is accompanied by severe vomiting and diarrhoea and which still kills many babies in this country is probably due to an unidentified virus spread from child to child on contaminated hands, feeding bottles, and food. The probability of its being spread in this way is supported by the observation that it very rarely affects breast fed babies.

The viruses responsible for the three infections so far described probably enter the body by way of the alimentary canal[1]:

1. The poliomyelitis virus may also be spread from infected persons by droplet infection.

many others are spread by droplet infection and enter through the respiratory tract. Viruses which enter the body in this way either remain localised in the respiratory system or spread to other parts of the body, often the skin.

Two frequent infections of the first type are the common cold and influenza. The common cold is caused by a virus present in the nasal secretions of an infected individual and spread by droplet infection: cold and damp may lower resistance or affect the mucous membrane of the nose and make it easier for the virus to establish itself. One of the most remarkable features of the influenza virus is its great variability. The first variant, type B, of the earliest virus recognised, type A, was identified in 1940; a new variant, the Asian virus, appeared in 1957 (see also Chapter I). The influenza virus causes an acute illness which varies greatly in severity. Characteristic symptoms due to the poisonous substances released from the damaged cells include raised temperature, pain in the back and limbs, and headache. In some cases the gastro-intestinal tract may be affected resulting in vomiting and diarrhoea, in others the nervous system is affected and delirium may occur.

Measles, German measles, chickenpox, and smallpox are four virus diseases which all follow the same general pattern: the infection begins in the upper respiratory tract, the viruses spread from here throughout the body and invade the cells of the skin. In measles the initial symptoms are those of a heavy cold and a dusky red raised rash begins to appear on the fourth day as the virus reaches the skin; in German measles the cold is slighter and there is marked enlargement of the lymph glands in the back of the neck while the rash is bright pink. The early invasion of the body by the chickenpox virus is rarely accompanied by any symptoms, the first sign is usually the appearance of the rash when the virus reaches and multiplies in the skin: in smallpox, however, the patient is often gravely ill for some three or four days before the rash appears. In both diseases, as already described, characteristic pustular lesions develop as the virus destroys the skin tissue. In chickenpox the pustules form rapidly and come out in crops, appearing first on the trunk where they are heavier than on the face and limbs. In smallpox the rash appears first on the face and limbs and is heavier here than on the trunk, and the pustules, which take much longer to develop, all appear simultaneously.

The relationship between chickenpox and shingles has long been a matter of interest. It was suggested as early as 1892 that both diseases were due to the same organism; a suggestion which has since been confirmed and the responsible virus identified. It is generally agreed that the virus causes shingles in an individual who has already had an attack of chickenpox and who therefore has some degree of immunity. The attack may, then, be due to reinfection or to the reactivation of the latent chickenpox virus which has been present ever since the initial attack. Why reactivation is unlikely to occur more than once is uncertain.

The mumps virus travels from the throat, where it enters the body, to the salivary glands (most often the parotid gland) and other glands, such as the testis in adult males. Extensive swelling of the affected glands follows a few days of general malaise.

In all these virus diseases the accompanying symptoms – fever, weakness, and often severe headache and prostration – are due to poisoning of the body by the products which damaged cells form as viruses destroy them.

A virus disease which departs somewhat from the general pattern is herpes. The herpes virus affects the skin of the lips causing the development of a blister which breaks down to form an encrusted sore. Although the sore heals in a day or two the condition is likely to recur and the sufferer may expect a crop of 'cold sores' every time particular conditions – a cold wind, excessive sunshine, a cold in the head – are experienced.

The primary infection with the herpes virus takes place in infancy: children over five years of age do not appear to be susceptible. This primary infection which causes an acute mouth condition, is contracted from saliva: if a herpes patient kisses a baby or contaminates with his saliva objects which the baby then puts in his mouth, the virus enters through any minute abrasion in the tongue, gums, or cheek lining. The infection clears up in about three weeks, but the virus has entered the deep, actively-growing cells of the skin in the infected area and here it remains for life, multiplying at the same rate as the skin cells, its rate of growth corresponding exactly with that of these cells. In this condition the virus remains indefinitely. Some change in conditions, as described above, can at any time act as a stimulant to virus growth: rapid multiplication begins, skin cells are destroyed and a typical cold sore develops. Sores are always in the same place; spread of the virus to adjacent cells is prevented by antibodies in the blood (see Chapter IV) produced at the time of the primary infection and reinforced at each subsequent one.

Viruses and tumours

Ever since viruses were first discovered their possible relationship to cancer has been a matter of interest. The demonstration of the presence of a virus in a tumour does not necessarily mean that it *causes* it: this is true only if a cell-free extract of the tumour is capable of inducing cancer in another animal. Early work was confined to tumours in birds, especially the domestic fowl, and at least eighteen types of tumour have been shown to be caused by viruses.

It has also been shown that tumours in certain mammals are due to virus invasion of the cells. The most important of these, known as polyoma virus, causes numerous types of tumours in various strains of mice and is also capable of infecting hamsters. Some mouse leukaemias have also been shown to be due to virus infection.

The position at present is that the electron microscope has revealed the presence of virus-like particles in many animal tumours and in some cases – mouse leukaemias and the polyoma tumours – the virus has been demonstrated to be the cause of the disease.

So far, little progress has been made in the study of the possible viral cause of human cancer. Perhaps the most interesting breakthrough was the demonstration in 1964 by Dr Harris at Mill Hill of a virus associated with leukaemia in human patients. The virus was present in the bone marrow of ten out of twenty-five patients with leukaemia and not in marrow examined from any individual without the disease. It must be stressed, however, that there is no proof whatsoever that the virus *causes* the disease, only that it appears to be associated with it.

Two further interesting suggestions have been made about the possible connection between viruses and cancer. The human body is known to harbour a large number of apparently harmless viruses, often called 'viruses in search of a disease'. It may be that a mutant form of the virus induced by some change in its immediate environment may render it cancer-producing. Or it may be that the same change activates a latent virus to cancer-producing activity. Perhaps the so-called carcinogens, which research shows are possible cancer-inducing agents, provide this environment for mutation or activation of a virus already present in the cells.

If cancer does prove to be a virus infection then a new weapon of attack may be available to us – that of virus interference. Recently the discovery of a tumour-destroying virus was reported from the Middlesex Hospital Medical School: when a solution of this virus, isolated from certain mouse tumours, is injected into a cancerous mouse, it begins to destroy the tumours which in many cases disappear altogether. The injected virus appears to be completely harmless to the mouse treated even when large doses are used.

Rickettsiae

The Rickettsiae are a group of rod-shaped organisms which differ from bacilli in that, like viruses, they are intracellular parasites and live only within the cells of susceptible hosts, normally in the lining cells of the intestinal tracts of various arthropod animals, especially fleas and lice. They can, however, like viruses, be grown in tissue culture and in the cells of the yolk sacs of chick embryos.

Although the normal hosts of the Rickettsias are the arthropods, some can cause severe infections in man when introduced into his tissues, usually by a bite. Typhus fever is one of the most important of these Rickettsial diseases. As already explained (Chapter I), typhus fever is spread by the body louse. The Rickettsiae multiply in the intestinal cells of the louse and large numbers of them are excreted in the saliva and faeces. In this way they may be introduced into man when he scratches himself or when the louse bites him. Once in the human tissues the Rickettsiae multiply and invade the blood vessels of the skin, the heart muscle, and the central nervous system. Within twelve days the infection is at its height: the patient complains of headache and chilling, and a rash appears accompanied by fever and stupor. In adults the mortality rate may be as high as forty per cent: in children the infection is usually mild.

The reservoir of the Rickettsiae causing endemic typhus is the rat: the organism is spread from rat to rat by the bite of the rat flea. It may be transferred to man from the rat in the same way and is then spread from man to man by the louse. Although the disease is milder than epidemic typhus, it is very widespread, and found in many different parts of the world.

The pathogenic protozoa

In temperate climates the majority of infectious diseases are caused by bacteria and viruses, but in tropical and subtropical zones pathogenic protozoa constitute a major problem. Many of these parasites are of particular biological interest on account of their complicated life histories and, as has already been discussed in Chapter I, many of the diseases which they cause are of great economic and social importance.

The pathogenic protozoa are amongst the smallest members of the group, the malarial parasite, for example, is no bigger than a large bacterium. The majority of protozoa are free living animals. They are found everywhere where there is a supply of moisture and of the still smaller micro-organisms upon which they feed: anyone who has made even an elementary study of the animal population of fresh water ponds and ditches must be familiar with the best known members of the group, Amoeba and Paramecium. Many protozoa find ideal living conditions in the alimentary canals of other animals: the gut of every vertebrate species has its own resident protozoal fauna; at least twelve different species inhabit the intestine of man. Here in the gut many protozoa find a rich supply of bacteria upon which they feed, causing no harm to their hosts. Others, however, have ceased to feed on the intestinal bacteria and have invaded the tissues of the host: there is considerable evidence that it is from these invaders that the pathogenic forms have evolved.

Parasitic members of two classes of protozoa, the Rhizopoda and the Mastigophora – more familiar examples of which are Amoeba and Euglena – are capable of causing disease in man. The most important of these parasites and the diseases which they cause are shown in Table 3.

Reference to the table shows that while some parasitic protozoa are transferred directly from host to host, in others, as has already been referred to in Chapter I, an insect or arthropod vector is involved in the spread.

In many parts of the tropics amoebic dysentery produces considerable sickness and suffering. The cause of the disease is

Entamoeba hystolytica. The adult animal is found in the large intestine of man where it may live quite harmlessly, feeding on the bacteria which are normally present. It may, however, under certain little-understood conditions attach itself to, and digest its way into, the lining of the intestine causing ulceration and haemorrhage.

Class	Parasite	Disease	Method of transmission
Rhizopoda	Entamoeba hystolytica	Amoebic dysentery	Direct
	Plasmodium vivax	Tertian malaria	Indirect by insect vector-mosquito
	Plasmodium falciparum	Malignant malaria	
	Plasmodium malariae	Quartan malaria	
	Plasmodium ovale	Tertian malaria	
Mastigophora	Trypanosoma gambiense	Sleeping sickness	Indirect by vector-tse-tse fly bug
	Trypanosoma rhodesiense		
	Trypanosoma cruzi		
	Leishmania donovani	Kala-azar	Indirect by insect vector-sandfly
	Leishmania tropica	Baghdad sore	

TABLE 3. Pathogenic protozoa

The adult animal divides repeatedly by binary fission and this leads to a rapid increase in the severity of the infection. The adult feeding form is, however, unable to survive when passed out of the body in the faeces and transmission to a new host is effected by a form encased in a protective cyst. In the encysted form the parasite may be swallowed by a new host. The contents of the cyst divide up to form eight small individuals which are set free into the intestine when the cyst wall is digested: no intermediate host is involved.

The tragic effects of malaria and the steps taken to bring it under control have already been described in Chapter I; a brief account of the causal protozoa, various species of the genus Plasmodium, follows.

Four different species of Plasmodium cause malaria in man (Table 3). The parasites are introduced into man by the bite of an infected mosquito and live within his liver and red blood cells, where for some time they multiply asexually. Finally, however, they produce sexual forms which alone are capable of infecting mosquitoes when these feed on blood. Within the bodies of the mosquitoes sexual reproduction results in the production of the form of the parasite capable of transmitting the disease to man.

The mosquitoes which are the intermediate hosts of all four species of Plasmodium all belong to the genus Anopheles. Only the female Anophelines suck blood, males feed on fruit juices and therefore do not transmit the disease. The life cycles of all four species of Plasmodium are basically the same; the description given below refers particularly to Plasmodium vivax, the species which causes benign tertian malaria.

The infective individuals which are introduced into man are minute spindle-shaped cells, many thousands of which may be injected into the blood when the female mosquito feeds. They are then carried in the blood to the liver where they enter into and feed upon the cells. Within each infected liver cell the parasite then divides up to form a number of tiny new individuals; up to 40,000 may be produced in this way in a few days. These individuals now leave the liver cells and each enters a red blood corpuscle within which the whole process is repeated: sixteen or thirty-two Plasmodia are formed within each red cell. The corpuscle is completely destroyed during this process and when it disintegrates the parasites are liberated into the plasma and are free to enter other red cells within which the whole process is repeated yet again.

Eventually the phase of asexual reproduction is over and each of the last-formed parasites grows into a new type of either male or female individual within the red corpuscle which it infects. These sexual forms, though incapable of further development in man, are infective to the mosquito. When the female mosquito sucks blood from a malaria patient only these sexual individuals survive; all other forms of the parasite are destroyed. Within the stomach of the mosquito the male and female cells give rise to male and female gametes: fertilisation results in the formation of a zygote. The zygote develops into a motile organism which bores through the gut wall, settles down on the outside of the stomach and grows into a blister-like cyst. Within the cyst repeated division of the contents results in the production of a large number of new infective individuals capable of survival in man. When the cyst on the stomach wall of the mosquito bursts these individuals are set free into the body cavity, reach and enter the salivary glands and are injected into man when the mosquito next feeds on human blood.

The malaria patient suffers from repeated 'attacks' – bouts of shivering followed by fever and culminating in a period of profuse sweating – which occur when the red corpuscles burst and release into the plasma, together with a fresh crop of parasites, the disintegrating products of the red cells. The patient becomes sensitised to these substances and the symptoms represent an allergic reaction (page 100). In Plasmodium vivax the bursting of the corpuscles takes place every third day and the disease it causes, which is of moderate severity, is called benign tertian malaria.

The frequency of the 'attacks' varies with the plasmodium species involved as shown in Table 4 below.

Species	Length of asexual cycle	Frequency of fever bouts	Type of malaria	Nature of disease
P. vivax	48 hours	About every 3rd day	Benign tertian	Moderate severity
P. falciparum	Less regular, about 48 hours	About every 3rd day	Malignant	Very severe, often fatal
P. malariae	72 hours	About every 4th day	Quartan	Mild
P. ovale	48 hours	About every 3rd day	Tertian	Mildest of al

TABLE 4. The pathogenic plasmodia

The condition may be complicated if, as often happens, the patient suffers a series of successive infections which may result in daily, or even twice daily 'attacks'. This is especially true of infections by P. falciparum, and the 'attacks' may become irregular or continuous.

'Attacks' do not begin until after the incubation period during which the parasites are multiplying in the blood. The length of the incubation period and the duration of the subsequent infection vary with the species of Plasmodium involved. Relapses may occur for several years (Table 5).

Species	Incubation period	Duration of infection	Relapses
P. vivax	9 to 17 days	2 to 4 weeks	Up to 3 years
P. falciparum	8 to 14 days	2 weeks	2 to 9 months
P. malariae	About 18 days	1 to 2 months	Up to 20 years
P. ovale	9 to 17 days	A few days	None

TABLE 5. Types of malaria

Plasmodium vivax is the most widely distributed of the four species: its sexual phase takes place at relatively lower temperatures and it predominates in temperate regions occurring as far north as Southern Sweden and as far south as Queensland. Plasmodium falciparum is found chiefly in tropical and sub-tropical zones and is rare in temperate regions, while

Plasmodium malariae is widespread but localised in Europe, Asia, southern U.S.A., South America, and Central and West Africa. Plasmodium ovale occurs in East and West Africa, Russia, Asia, and in Central and South America (Fig. 4).

The trypanosomes

The trypanosomes are members of the class Mastigophora, a class characterised by the possession of a whip-like flagellum. Three species of trypanosomes are parasitic in man and cause the disease known technically as trypanosomiasis and more familiarly as sleeping sickness. All three species have indirect life-histories and in all cases the vector is a blood sucking insect or arthropod. Trypanosoma gambiense and Trypanosoma rhodesiense, both of which, as their names suggest, are found in Africa, are transmitted by tse-tse flies; Trypanosoma cruzi, which comes from South America, is transmitted by blood-sucking bugs.

Trypanosoma gambiense and Trypanosoma rhodesiense have many features in common and will be considered first. In the body of the infected man the trypanosomes live first in the blood, causing a feverish condition in the patient, but soon they make their way to the lymphatic system where they produce a state of chronic inflammation. Finally the parasites reach the cerebro-spinal fluid and then the apathy, incoordination of the muscles, emaciation, and sleepiness characteristic of the disease become evident. Death eventually results, caused either by the parasites directly or as the result of some secondary infection, such as pneumonia, which the patient contracts in his weakened condition. Trypanosoma gambiense causes a form of the disease which is slow to develop, the patient often surviving for several years; the sickness resulting from infection by Trypanosoma rhodesiense is rapidly fatal, the patient rarely living for more than twelve months.

Trypanosoma cruzi, the parasite which causes trypanosomiasis in America, differs considerably from the two African species. The adult parasites live not in the blood but in the phagocytic cells of the spleen, liver, bone marrow, lymphatic glands, and often in the cardiac muscle. Within the cells the trypanosomes pass through a complicated series of stages during which they multiply rapidly and eventually produce forms which leave the cells and enter the blood. When a bug feeds on an infected human being these forms are sucked in with the blood and after a complicated series of changes in the food canal of the bug, give rise to forms capable of reinfecting man. The bug often defaecates while feeding and when this happens infective individuals get onto the skin of the man on whom the bug is feeding. The parasites then make their way into the body either through the wound made by the bug or other abrasions made by the victim when he scratches. Infection usually begins round the mouth, nostrils, and eyes, the places where the bug most often bites. The parasites enter the phagocytic cells of the skin and underlying muscles, multiply rapidly, enter the blood and travel to the heart and other organs. The resulting disease may be mild and clear up completely or severe in which case it may be acute and prove rapidly fatal. Often, however, the disease becomes chronic, death occurring only after a long illness.

The parasitic worms

Parasitic worms are responsible for an enormous amount of suffering, especially in tropical parts of the world. Members of two phyla, the Nemathelminthes and the Platyhelminthes, are the chief culprits.

The disease-causing Nemathelminthes belong to the class Nematoda and are known as the round worms. They are smooth, cylindrical creatures, varying in length from a few millimetres to several centimetres, which live parasitically in various parts of the body of man and other animals, bringing disease and death to millions of human beings in many parts of the world. Some are spread directly from one human individual to another, others have a complicated life history, and like the protozoan parasite, Plasmodium, must live for a time in the body of one or even two other hosts before their life-cycle can be completed.

One of the most pernicious of all Nematodes is the hook worm and this parasite is selected for detailed description as a representative member of the group.

All species of hook worm live in the small intestine. Although there are minor differences between the various forms, their life-histories and the effect which they have upon the infected man are essentially similar: the following description applies specifically to Ancylostoma duodenale.

Superficially Ancylostoma duodenale is a small harmless-looking creature, a greyish-white thread between eight and thirteen millimetres in length, but its evil potentialities lie in the tiny sharp teeth-like cutting plates which lie within its small sucker-like mouth. Into this mouth the worm sucks a plug of the delicate lining of the small intestine: with its teeth it bites off portions of this plug to use as food or scrapes away the lining until it erodes the tiny capillaries and sucks out blood. To promote blood flow and prevent clotting the worm injects a powerful anticoagulent into the damaged tissues. Observations on infected dogs show that each worm can remove as much as half a millilitre of blood in a day: heavy infestation, which is common, may therefore lead to very considerable loss of blood. The worm probably actually feeds upon the tissues of the eroded intestinal lining: the blood, which passes quickly through the body, is probably taken as a source of haemoglobin to assist the worm in its respiration.

The adult worms live in the small intestine and the eggs which the female lays pass out with the faeces. The first larval form which hatches out of the egg feeds on faecal bacteria, grows rapidly and moults twice to produce a second and finally a third larval form. The third larva is a small active worm about half a millimetre long and it represents the infective stage of the life cycle. It, and it alone, can infect a new host, entering either through the mouth or by penetrating the skin. From the site of entry the third larva is carried in the blood to the lungs where it bores its way out of the capillaries, enters the air-sacs and travels along the bronchi to reach the throat. During this journey the third larva develops into a fourth larva which when swallowed grows into an adult worm in the small intestine. It is estimated that one hundred hook worms will cause disease in a child and five hundred in a healthy adult, though a poorly nourished individual may show symptoms if infected by as few as twenty-five.

Hook worms are not primarily killers but the serious anaemia which they cause in the host leads to chronic debility and loss of efficiency. It is estimated that at least 450 million people in different parts of the world are infected by hook worms: it is obvious, therefore, that the parasite has serious social and economic consequences. Although the hook worms can be removed with medical help from the body of the patient and

Name	Site of infection	Effect	Intermediate host
The Round worm			
Ascaris lumbricoides	Small intestine	Inflammation and obstruction of intestine, jaundice	None
The Pin or Thread worm			
Enterobius vermicularis	Caecum, appendix, colon, intestine	Discomfort and irritation	None
The Trichina worm			
Trichinella spiralis	Adult—small intestine Larva—muscles	Diarrhoea Stiffness, rheumatic pains	Pig, dog, cat Fox, rat
The Filarial worms			
Wuchereria bancrofti	Lymph vessels and glands	Elephantiasis	Mosquito
Wuchereria malayi			Mosquito
Onchocera volvulus			Blackfly
Loa Loa	Subcutaneous tissue, eye	Calabar swelling	Flies of the genus Chrysop
The Guinea worm			
Dracunculus medensis	Connective tissue	Rash, nausea, vomiting, diarrhoea, giddiness	Cyclops
The Hook worms			
Ancylostoma duodenale	Intestine	Chronic debility and anaemia	None
Ancylostoma braziliensis			
Ancylostoma ceylanicum			
Necator americanus			

TABLE 6. The parasitic nematodes

PLATE 9: Miracle drug—the effects

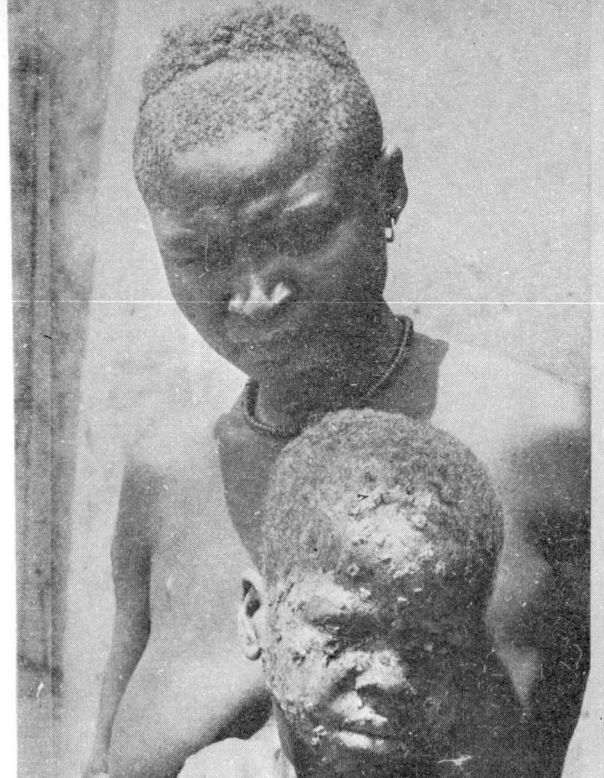

(a) Five-year-old Ebu has yaws

(b) Ebu ten days after a single injection of long-acting penicillin provided by a W.H.O.-assisted team

PLATE 10: The full effects of atmospheric pollution are appreciated only when buildings are cleaned and restored. Two views of premises in Wood's Circus, Bath

PLATE 11:
Human albinos

A Zulu

Three Europeans

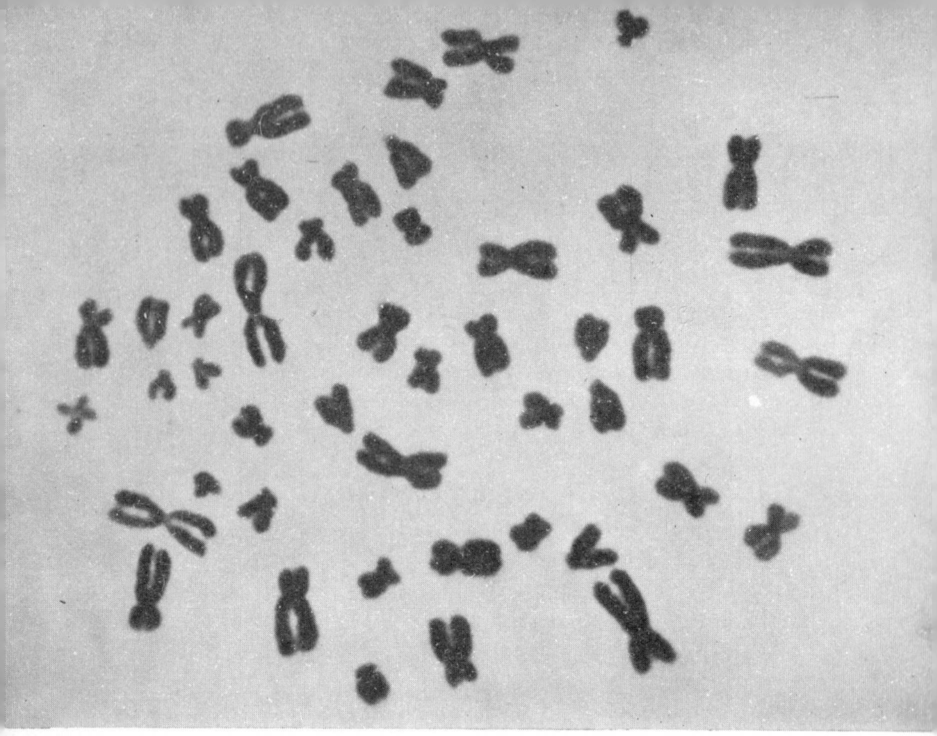

PLATE 12: Normal and abnormal human chromosomes. (*a*) *Above*, Normal female (46); (*b*) *Below*, Female mongol (47)

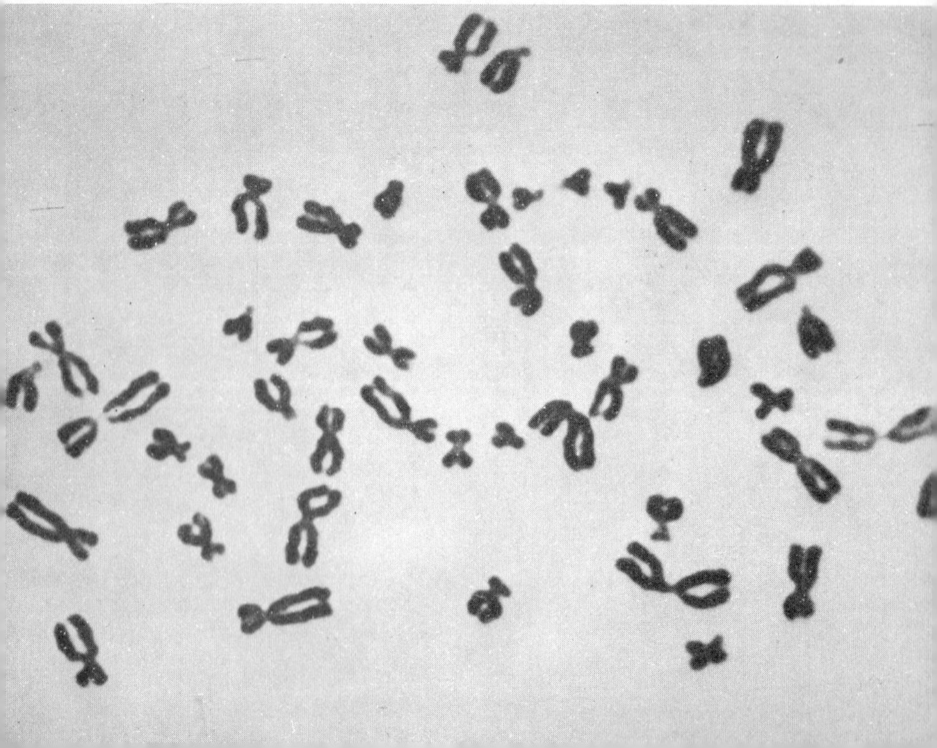

the anaemia successfully treated, it is obviously much more desirable to take all possible steps to prevent the initial infection. How this may be done is considered later.

A brief summary of the other important parasitic Nematodes, the life-histories of most of which involve one or more alternative hosts, is given in Table 6.

Disease-causing Platyhelminthes are flukes belonging to the class Trematoda, and tape worms, members of the class Cestoda. The bodies of all flukes and tapeworms are extensively flattened and they are provided with hooks or suckers or both with which they attach themselves to their hosts.

At least ten different species of flukes are parasitic in the human body, some living in the intestine, some in the liver and lungs, and others in the blood. The most important flukes parasitic in man are shown in Table 7 below.

Name	Common name	Site of infection
The Intestinal flukes		
Fasciolepsis buskii	The large intestinal fluke	Small intestine
Heterophyes heterophyes		Small intestine
Metagonimus yokagawi		Intestine
The Liver flukes		
Fasciola hepatica	The common liver fluke	Liver
Opisthorchis sinensis	The oriental liver fluke	Liver
Opisthorchis felinius	The cat liver fluke	Liver
The Lung flukes		
Paragonimus westermanii	The oriental lung fluke	Lungs
The Blood flukes		
Schistosoma haematobium	The urinary blood fluke	Blood vessels of bladder
Schistosoma mansonii	The intestinal blood fluke	Blood vessels of large intestine
Schistosoma japonicum	The oriental blood fluke	Blood vessels of small intestine

TABLE 7. The parasitic flukes

All of the flukes, like some of the Nematodes, have a complicated life-history involving at least one and often two hosts other than man. Two important members of the group, the intestinal fluke and the blood fluke, are selected for detailed description.

The intestinal flukes

Some ten million people in China, Malaya, Borneo, Assam, and Bengal are estimated to have the parasite Fasciolepsis buskii in the small intestine. The adult fluke which is a relatively large animal, up to 7·5 centimetres in length, is shaped like a fleshy leaf and is attached by suckers to the lining of the host's intestine. The presence of the fluke causes inflammation and ulceration: a heavy infestation – up to 3,000 have been removed from the intestine of a single individual – causes severe illness and may be fatal. The fertilised eggs leave the human body in the faeces and the eggs hatch in damp surroundings. The larvae, called miracidia, which emerge continue their development only in the tissues of certain aquatic snails. The miracidia bore their way into the body of the snail and within its tissues each passes through a complicated series of larval stages to produce finally an infective stage, the cercaria. The cercaria leave the snails and settle down on the leaves and stems of various aquatic plants. Here they encyst and if the plants are edible and are eaten raw by man, the cysts rupture and the cercariae enter the alimentary canal and develop into adult flukes.

The blood flukes

Three species of blood flukes cause the disease known as schistosomiasis or bilharziasis in man. Schistosoma haematobium, Schistosoma mansonii, and Schistosoma japonicum live in the blood vessels of the urinary bladder, the large intestine, and the small intestine respectively. The first two species are widespread in tropical areas of the world; the third is confined to certain areas in Japan, China, and adjacent areas in the Far East. The adult flukes are minute flattened, leaf-like animals provided with suckers and possibly hooks or clamps with which they attach themselves to the tissues of the host.

The blood flukes are most unusual parasites in that in all three species the damage to the host is caused not by the adult worms but by the fertilised eggs laid by the adult females in the small blood vessels of the organ which they infect. The eggs, which are laid in enormous numbers and literally fill the vessels involved, each bear a pointed spine: the irritation which this causes leads to severe inflammation of the affected organ. Enzymes produced by the egg destroy the tissues and the eggs eventually escape into the bladder or intestine and leave the body in the urine or faeces. The pattern of the life-cycle is similar to that of Fasciolepsis buskii. Each egg contains a delicate ciliated miracidium whose continued existence depends upon its entry into a specific type of aquatic snail. After boring its way into the snail, the miracidium gives rise eventually to a large number of very active cercariae which escape from the snail into the water. These cercariae, however, unlike those of the intestinal and liver flukes, do not encyst, but are able actively to penetrate the human skin wherever they come in contact with it. From the skin's blood vessels which they have penetrated, the cercariae are carried in the blood to the liver. Here they mature into adult flukes and thence pass to the vessels of the organ finally affected.

The tape worms

The tape worm differs from the fluke in that its body consists of a chain of segments or proglottides budded off from a tiny head or scolex. The chain may be short, consisting of three or four segments only, or of enormous length, made up of as many as 4,000 proglottides.

The beef tape worm is selected as a typical member of the group. The worm is found in man all over the world, but is now rare in this country. It is estimated that there may be as many as thirty million people acting as hosts to the tape worm: once established, the worm may survive in the intestine for as long as ten years. The adult worm lives in the intestine attached to the lining by the scolex. Its presence may have little effect upon the host or may cause abdominal pain, weakness, loss of weight, nausea, restlessness, and a marked increase in appetite. In a few people the poisonous substances released by the worm may cause convulsions. The scolex may also injure the lining of the intestine and infection of the wound lead to ulceration.

The tape worm has an interesting and complicated life history. The terminal proglottides, full of ripe eggs, become detached from the chain, pass out of the body in the faeces and, as the tissues of the proglottid disintegrate, the eggs are set free. Within each proglottid a characteristic six-hooked or hexanth larva is formed but development goes no further unless the egg is swallowed by a suitable host. The intermediate hosts are various members of the cattle family. In the alimentary canal of the second host the egg hatches and the hexanth larva bores its way into the blood or lymph system and is carried to the muscles. In the muscles the larva settles down and grows into a small bladder-like creature, the hydatid cyst, within which a new larval form, the cysticercus develops. No further development of the cysticercus takes place unless the tissue containing it is eaten by man while it is alive: this happens if man eats infected beef raw. In the alimentary canal of man the cysticercus then develops into an adult tape worm.

In order to bring the parasitic worms under control, the life cycle must be broken at some vulnerable point.

Elimination of hook worm infection depends upon interruption of the life cycle either at the egg stage or at the infective third larval stage. Man can become infected only when he comes in contact with soil contaminated with human faeces containing the third larval stage. The skin of the hands and feet is most often exposed to infection in this way: the larvae usually enter through the soft skin between the toes or covering the ankles. The most effective method of control is therefore to prevent the deposition of human faeces anywhere where it is likely to produce larvae which may contact human skin. The provision and proper use of adequate sanitation has eradicated the disease from many parts of the world; in other parts good sanitation has not yet been, or cannot be, provided. Because the third larval stage thrives only in warm, moist soil the disease is primarily one of the tropics: it is just these areas where there are many countries in which sanitation is primitive, where the climate makes footwear, and, for children, clothing of any kind unnecessary and where human excreta is often used untreated as manure and deposited indiscriminately on the ground where adults walk and children play. Hookworm infections remain widespread and serious where modern hygiene and education have so far failed.

As in the round worms, the most effective method of controlling flukes is to prevent the contamination of water by the faeces of man and other animals. The snails can be destroyed to prevent the miracidia from continuing their development. Destruction may be brought about in a variety of ways. The water may be disinfected with chemicals or the leaves among which the snails live may be cleared away. Whole areas of snail-infested waters may be drained: this is not always practicable as the life of some areas depends upon its irrigation system. Drinking water may be boiled, chlorinated, or filtered to kill or remove the cercariae. This is an effective control only where cercariae are taken in through the mouth. As in the prevention of hook worm infection the skin may be protected from the infective larvae – the cercariae – which would otherwise penetrate it, by footwear, and, when appropriate, by rubber gloves. Infection by species in which the cercariae encyst on water plants may be prevented by refraining from eating fresh, raw plants from contaminated waters.

As with the hook worms the countries where flukes flourish are often those where sanitation is primitive and the population ignorant of the elementary rules of hygiene. Control is at the best difficult and only partially effective.

The control of tape worm infections demands not only a thorough knowledge of the life cycle of the worm but also of the mode of life of the human beings concerned: their habits, social activities, and especially their feeding habits. Efficient sewage disposal ensures that human faeces do not contaminate ground where domestic animals feed: careful inspection and thorough cooking of all meat prevents human beings from ingesting live cysticerci.

CHAPTER III

The Control of Infection

It is evident from the preceding chapters that infection is one of the chief hazards to health. Not only is infectious disease still a major cause of death, but it is also a grave menace to normal, healthy development. Many infections of childhood are seriously debilitating and after-effects may persist for years, adversely affecting development at a vital time. Some may leave behind a permanent legacy of ill-health or disability. The control of infection is obviously of major importance in the health programme of any community.

The scientific study and eventual control of infection was made possible by the discovery in the 1860's of the relationship between germs and disease, and during the last hundred years much progress has been made in bringing infectious diseases under control. The ultimate aim is theoretically to eliminate every pathogenic germ from the whole surface of the globe but no disease-causing germ has yet been totally eradicated in this way. Thirty years ago, after a long and heroic struggle, hope was high that yellow fever might be totally eliminated by complete destruction of its mosquito vector. As described in Chapter I, this hope was dashed by the discovery that animal reservoirs of the disease exist deep in the jungles and spread by jungle mosquitoes. The hope of total extermination of these is very slender indeed.

But although total elimination is apparently impossible, many diseases have been wiped out over large areas. Smallpox, plague, malaria, and rabies are four diseases once common and now no longer endemic in this country, though all four are still rife in other parts of the world. The control of the first three has already been considered. Rabies, a disease spread from dogs to man by the bite of an infected animal, was stamped out in Britain over fifty years ago. In 1897 regulations were enforced under which all infected dogs were destroyed, all other dogs in affected areas were muzzled for the next six months and all dogs entering the country were quarantined. In two years, except in one isolated area, rabies had disappeared. There has only been one small outbreak since, started by a dog smuggled by air into this country. The only item of the regulation which needs to be, and still is, enforced today is the quarantine for all immigrant dogs. In other parts of the world, however, especially in the tropics, rabies claims hundreds of victims every year.

It is important to remember that unless a disease is eliminated from the whole globe, then constant vigilance is necessary in the clear areas to hold it in check. The people in these areas, never having been exposed to the particular infection have no naturally acquired immunity and the position thus becomes doubly serious. In this country opinion has tended to harden against compulsory smallpox vaccination: the incubation period is short, about seven days; any potential patient will develop the disease during the long sea voyage from contaminated areas in the East and all contacts can be vaccinated. But the development of air travel has completely altered the position: the journey from the East takes only two or three days and a traveller who has contracted the disease before embarkation may have spent several days in this country before the symptoms appear. It would be impossible to trace all contacts and emergency vaccination might not prevent a serious outbreak. The widespread outbreak which occurred in 1962 was a sharp reminder that this is indeed so.

Statistical analysis shows that both the incidence of and the death rate from infectious disease is greatly affected by social conditions. Overcrowding obviously favours the spread of respiratory infections; poor nutrition, the outcome of both poverty and ignorance, lowers resistance to infection and decreases chances of survival; dirt and inadequate sanitation facilitate the spread of faeces-borne diseases; ignorance and neglect lead to failure to detect the onset of a disease in its early stages and delay in obtaining advice. The prevention of infection is obviously not only a medical, but also a social and economic problem.

It is evident from the preceding chapters that for those working to bring infectious diseases under control, knowledge of their causes and methods of spread is of vital importance: some measure of success has been achieved without this knowledge but the methods adopted are bound to be empirical. On the other hand, possession of these facts does not inevitably mean success; nevertheless it makes it possible to instigate a determined scientific attack upon the disease in question. Nowhere is this better illustrated than in the attack upon diseases spread by contaminated food and water, by the bites of animals, and by direct entry through the skin. In so many instances the knowledge is there – what is lacking is the ability or opportunity to apply it to the full.

The control of food- and water-borne diseases

The pathogenic bacteria and viruses which invade the body by way of the alimentary system are spread by faecal contamination of water, milk, food, and cooking utensils which may be contaminated directly or indirectly by fingers or flies. Strict supervision of those engaged in the food trade, and the care taken by all those engaged in the preparation of food, whether in the home, canteen, or restaurant, have decreased enormously the incidence of typhoid fever in this country but the germ has not been eliminated. It still lingers on in the bodies of many unwitting 'carriers' and they are always a potential source of danger. Frequently a typhoid outbreak can be traced to failure on the part of a carrier to comply with the regulations laid down for safeguarding health.

Every hot summer there are in this country mild and often severe outbreaks of food poisoning and minor food infections. Poliomyelitis outbreaks and epidemics of gastro-enteritis are often associated with the warm summer months. Such outbreaks may be the outcome of inadequate standards of food handling and methods of rubbish disposal. As long as scientific waste disposal units are a luxury the fly-ridden dustbin will remain a potential source of danger.

As already described rigid control of sanitation and of drinking water supplies has been instrumental in the elimination of cholera. The cholera bacterium is effectively destroyed by chlorination: it is important to remember that the poliomyelitis virus survives such treatment. It is this which makes the swimming bath a potential danger during a poliomyelitis epidemic.

Tuberculin tested herds of cows and the practice of pasteurising milk have been very effective in stamping out bovine tuberculosis which is now rare in this country (Plate 6).

The control of insect-borne infections

The way in which an infection which is spread by the bite of an insect or arthropod vector can be brought under control by mounting a full-scale attack upon the vector has already been described. Plague, typhus, yellow fever, malaria, and sleeping sickness have all been brought under at least partial control in this way. Relentless war on fleas, lice, mosquitoes, and tse-tse flies has been waged successfully and although the diseases which they spread have not been totally eliminated at least they have been partially controlled and contained. As already described in Chapter I, the problem is now a social and economic one.

The control of venereal disease

In theory, it would appear that the control of venereal disease is a simple matter; in practice, it is very difficult. Venereal syphilis is predominantly a disease of urban areas which spreads to rural communities with the mass migrations which accompany poverty, war, and territorial occupation. The marked increase in incidence which inevitably accompanies any major war is followed by a decline with the return of the stability associated with peace and normal economic and social conditions. The disease can best be controlled by attacking it in three inter-related ways: by the systematic identification of cases, by the prolonged treatment of these cases once they have been identified, and by strenuous educational efforts. A major problem remains in the continued existence of reservoirs of syphilitic infection in vast areas of the world, where control activities are difficult. There are estimated to be many millions of cases in these areas.

The control of respiratory infections

While some control can be exercised over contact with water, food, and insect-borne diseases, avoidance of contact with respiratory infections is a much more difficult problem. Organisms harboured in the respiratory passages will be present in the saliva and carried out in the breath especially during coughing, sneezing, and shouting. Visible droplets settle quickly and rarely spread infection but small ones remain suspended, the water evaporates and the organisms are left behind in the organic residue. They are taken into the nose and throat of another individual with the inspired air and lead to respiratory infection. As long as any droplet-spread disease is endemic in the community every individual is exposed to infection. The spread of such infections is obviously favoured by poor living conditions, and susceptibility is often increased by undernourishment. The classic disease of overcrowding and undernourishment is pulmonary tuberculosis.

Prophylaxis and artificially induced immunity

It is obvious that it may not always be possible to avoid contact with disease-causing organisms, even if we know how they are spread.

We may have to go to malaria- or typhoid-infested countries where we cannot ensure that we will not be bitten by a mosquito or drink infected water. In this country, although we may feel reasonably safe from insect- and water-borne diseases, we cannot avoid contact with the germs of the air-borne infections – diphtheria and tuberculosis; chickenpox, measles and mumps; influenza and the common cold. Nor in our present state of knowledge can we adopt absolutely certain avoiding tactics against the poliomyelitis virus. So scientists have devised other methods of providing protection against those germs which cannot be avoided.

One way to deal with the infection before it gets a hold in the body is by using prophylactic drugs. Quinine, for example, has long been used to arrest the progress of malaria after infection; now it has largely been replaced by paludrine and chloroquin. Such prophylactic treatment, however, is not practicable as a general protective measure; it is effective only when an individual is known to have been infected with a specific germ as may happen in malaria and venereal syphilis. It is also essential in surgery, especially of the lung, to protect the rest of the body from the germs in the infected tissue.

Another and much more widely used protective measure, where elimination of the disease or its prevention by drug prophylaxis is not possible, is to encourage the development of immunity.

In order to understand the phenomenon of immunity, it is essential to know something of the way in which the body reacts when its tissues are injured or invaded.

Whenever tissue is injured, however slight the injury may be, foreign matter – invading micro-organisms and dead cells destroyed by the organisms or in any other way – are got rid of by a process known as phagocytosis. This is carried out by cells known as phagocytes.

Phagocytes are cells capable of amoeboid movement which are able to engulf and destroy cell debris and invading micro-organisms. They occur in both blood and connective tissue. Between 72 and 76% of the leucocytes or white corpuscles of the blood are phagocytic. By far the greater proportion of these (68–70% of the total of leucocytes) are large cells with lobed nuclei and coarsely granular cytoplasm. These are the polymorphonuclear leucocytes or polymorphs. They are very mobile and particularly active in the engulfing and destruction of micro-organisms. They are formed in the red bone marrow outside the blood vessels from primitive white cells or myeloblasts. When mature they migrate through the walls of the capillaries and enter the blood.

Phagocytic cells are also present in connective tissue; these include free and fixed histiocytes and mast cells. The free histiocytes, which are also called wandering cells or macrophages, are widely distributed and move freely about in the connective tissue. Mast cells, which are found in smaller numbers, manufacture the anticoagulant, heparin. The fixed histiocytes on the other hand have permanent positions in the body: they are found in serous membranes and in the lining of the internal spaces in the liver and spleen where they have a vital anti-infective role.

If the injured tissue is free from blood vessels then macrophages from the surrounding tissues accumulate in the area and devour the debris.

But phagocytes will accumulate much more rapidly in the damaged area if the blood plays some part in the reaction: phagocytes can then be brought quickly from all parts of the body. Such an involvement of the blood system occurs in almost all injuries and so phagocytosis becomes part of the complex process called inflammation. Inflammation – the familiar sign of injury in any tissue – involves a complicated sequence of reactions in the damaged area: some of these result in the visible and tangible symptoms – redness, heat, swelling, and pain, which, as rubor, calor, turgor, and dolor, have for centuries been described as the cardinal symptoms of the process.

Detailed study of events in the damaged area shows how these symptoms, and others which are not so readily appreciated, are brought about. Dilatation of the venules and then of the capillaries in the area leads to an accelerated and increased blood flow: this accounts for the redness and heat. An alteration in the nature of the capillary walls leads to their increased permeability; an increased effusion of tissue fluid takes place and swelling occurs as this accumulates. If sensory nerves are involved the area becomes painful. After a short while the blood flow slows down and the leucocytes 'stick' to the inner walls of the capillaries and then by an active movement known as diapedesis the blood phagocytes pass through the walls of the capillaries into the tissue fluid. At the same time macrophages migrate to the injured area: between them the phagocytes remove the dead tissue and any invading micro-organisms. Phagocytes themselves are killed in large numbers and eventually the damaged area becomes virtually filled with dead, disintegrating phagocytes and debris which form a foul-smelling, creamy liquid, pus. At the same time the infected area is effectively walled off from the surrounding living tissue by a barrier of connective tissue infiltrated with phagocytes and in this way the spread of germs is prevented. The pus-filled bag so formed is an abscess. Eventually the abscess disintegrates and discharges its pus: it may be very tiny and its eruption pass almost unnoticed or in more severe infections it may be of considerable size and require surgical treatment. When all the pus has drained away repair takes place.

Phagocytosis is most important in extracellular infections, those in which the organisms remain outside the cells. Extracellular infections include the majority of acute bacterial infections: chronic bacterial, virus, and protozoal infections are intracellular and phagocytosis is less effective. Phagocytosis is effective only when some rough surface is available: the cells trap the bacteria against the surface and engulf them. Such a surface is provided by the walls of the alveoli or the fibrin in a blood clot. Open cavities, such as the abdominal, pleural, and meningeal cavities all of which are fluid-filled, offer no solid surface and natural resistance to infection is lower. Abscesses too are fluid-filled: chemotherapy and draining are therefore necessary.

Although many infections of the body are effectively dealt

with locally, in the way described, this is not always so. Some bacteria, like the diphtheria bacillus, are usually unable, however inadequate the local defences, to spread from the tissue where they first invaded. The majority of micro-organisms, however, if they can resist the effects of the local reactions at their site of entry, are able to spread widely through the body. How successfully they do this depends upon a number of factors: the virulence of the invading germs, the strength of the attack, and the effectiveness of the local resistance. When a clinical attack of a disease, for example, measles, develops this indicates that the insufficient local defences of the throat have been overcome by a heavy dose of virulent viruses which have spread all over the body to produce their characteristic effects in the skin. In paralytic poliomyelitis local defences have been overcome and the virus has reached the anterior horn cells of the spinal cord.

In every case where a clinical attack of an infection develops the germs have overcome the local defences at the site of the infection and they, their toxins or the poisons produced as the result of their activity, have spread throughout the body. Once the germs have evaded the local defences, however, before the infection becomes general, several other defence barriers have to be broken down: general infection does not necessarily follow the defeat of the local defences. General blood poisoning does not inevitably follow the spread of staphylococci from a cut finger, even if these have already reached the upper arm. The lymph and circulatory systems may between them effectively prevent the invasion becoming general.

If the germs overcome the local defences they enter the lymph and pass along the lymph vessels to the lymph nodes where the fixed phagocytes engulf and destroy foreign particles. In addition, it is here that the other important leucocytes, the non-phagocytic lymphocytes are formed. These are small cells with relatively large rounded nuclei and little cytoplasm containing a few coarse granules. Here in the nodes where they originate, the lymphocytes perform their known functions – the inactivation of bacteria and of toxins. What happens to them when they enter the blood is unknown.

Lymphocytes and monocytes between them are able to inactivate and remove large numbers of micro-organisms: 99% of streptococci introduced into the lymph can be removed by passing through a lymph gland. It is probable that some germs reach the nearest glands in any infection but are effectively inactivated and removed so that there is no general infection. The more virulent germs, however, are able to dissolve the clotted lymph in the vessels and so reach the glands in large numbers. If the lymph vessels are superficial, as in the arm, a red line of inflammation may be seen marking the progress of the infection. The glands themselves, in the axilla, for example, following an infected cut finger, or in the neck accompanying a sore throat, may become inflamed and feel swollen and tender.

If the organisms pass the lymph glands they enter the blood. Now the fixed histiocytes in the liver and spleen become all important as the last elements capable of removing the germs and so preventing a general infection. If these defences too are evaded a clinical attack of the particular disease with its specific symptoms develops. It will be noted that blood phagocytes – the polymorphs and monocytes – are not important in overcoming general infections; their main function is to deal with local infections.

The pattern of a clinical infection

Many germs which invade the body are successfully dealt with by the body's defences and a general infection does not occur. Other germs, however, cannot be destroyed unaltered by the phagocytes. Also, as already stated, many bacteria, like the diphtheria bacillus, produce highly destructive toxins which if allowed to circulate in the blood do considerable damage to the tissues. When the body is invaded for the first time by a heavy dose of such virulent organisms, a clinical attack of the specific disease follows. The course of the attack follows a definite pattern. The onset of the disease, which may be sudden or slow, is accompanied by vague symptoms which give place to a period of illness with general and characteristic signs and symptoms. During this time the virulent germs have things all their own way and the phagocytes are unable to destroy them. The germs multiply rapidly and they and their toxins damage the cells. The germs may remain localised or they or their toxins or both, together with the abnormal products of cell disintegration, may be carried by the blood to all parts of the body. Cells are damaged temporarily or permanently, and the patient often feels extremely ill and may die. But the majority of infectious diseases are not fatal: soon the patient begins to get the better of the invaders, the toxins are rendered harmless, the symptoms abate and, unless permanent damage has been done to any particular cells, recovery is complete. The stages take a definite time for each specific disease: the doctor can say when the turning point will come and when recovery will be complete.

There is no evidence whatever that there is any change in the nature of the germs as they multiply within the body; recovery takes place because of a change in the body's reaction to these germs. These changes are due to the production in the blood of important chemical compounds which are called antibodies: these antibodies have the property of sticking to the surfaces of the germs. The virulent germ with its coating of antibody can now be dealt with by the phagocytes in exactly the same way as if it were non-virulent: the moment when this process begins to be effective marks the turning point of the disease and from then on the patient recovers. In the same way and at the same time, toxins are coated with antitoxin, rendered harmless and destroyed.

The production of specific antibody does not only make it possible for the body to overcome invasion by virulent germs but it also confers upon it an immunity to the particular infection. Antibody is formed abundantly in response to any particular invasion and any excess will remain: this will then deal with a fresh influx of the same type of germs into the blood. Furthermore, the tissues, 'educated' in the production of this particular antibody will produce it more rapidly and effectively should the same antigen[1] again enter the tissues. So effective is this production that it is rare for a patient to suffer twice from an infection like measles, chickenpox, or poliomyelitis where the organisms travel in the blood. In conditions like colds and influenza, however, where the infection gets a hold without the virus entering the blood, the antibodies, if present, are less likely to come in contact with the newly invading antigens: immunity in these cases is of short duration only and is due to the presence of antibodies in the film of moisture which covers the surfaces of the susceptible cells in the respiratory passages. This antibody

1. Foreign proteins which stimulate antibody formation are known as antigens (see page 95).

was formed in the lymph nodes in response to the presence there of virus which had spread from its site of entry but had found no susceptible cells to invade. The antibody conveyed in the lymph to the blood seeps through the walls of the capillaries into the film of moisture. As long as it remains it will prevent reinfection by the same organism but the immunity rarely lasts more than a few weeks.

We are now in a better position to understand how the induction of specific immunities by artificial means could be a most valuable protective measure against certain infections. The aim is to stimulate the body to produce its own antibodies against specific diseases. This must be achieved without causing harm to the tissues and without exposing the subject to any undue risks. The appropriate antigen must be obtained in a harmless form but also in such a condition that it will induce antibody formation. From the antigen a vaccine suitable for inoculation is then prepared.

Two methods of artificially inducing an active immunity of this type are in use. The subject may be inoculated with living germs of reduced virulence which while producing no dangerous symptoms will provoke antibody formation. Such attenuated organisms are used to provide immunity to smallpox, yellow fever, tuberculosis (the BCG vaccine), plague and poliomyelitis (the oral or 'sugar lump' vaccine). The introduction of live organisms into the body, however, always involves an element of risk. The vaccine cannot be sterilised, and may contain other pathogenic organisms with which it has been contaminated. Alternatively, a vaccine is prepared containing not attenuated, but dead, organisms which, while stimulating antibody formation, are themselves harmless. The appropriate organisms are killed, and, in an antiseptic fluid used as a vaccine to provide immunity to typhoid and paratyphoid fever, plague, whooping cough, cholera, typhus, and poliomyelitis (the Salk vaccine). When vaccines are prepared from dead organisms meticulous testing is essential to ensure that all such organisms have indeed been killed. Identification of the German measles virus in 1962 has led to extensive research into the preparation of a vaccine which would reduce the dangers of this disease to young women (see page 136).

A third type of vaccine is used when the symptoms of the disease are due not to the organisms themselves but to the toxins which they produce, as in diphtheria and tetanus: the aim is to induce the formation of antitoxin. Toxins obtained from a suitable culture of the bacteria are rendered non-poisonous by treatment with formalin and the toxoid so prepared is inoculated and stimulates the formation of antitoxin.

Protection can also be given to contacts who may be incubating a disease, or help to patients in the early stages of infection, by inoculating them with antibodies produced in the tissues of another human being or suitable animal host. This technique is successfully used to protect delicate or ill children who have been in contact with measles, those who have deep penetrating wounds which may be contaminated with the tetanus bacillus, and diphtheria contacts (see below). It is also used to help tetanus and diphtheria patients in the early stages of the disease. These foreign antibodies, however, provide only a short-lived passive immunity in contrast to the active immunity, which is of much longer duration, set up when the subject produces his own antibodies.

The control of diphtheria

The nature and cause of diphtheria have already been described. Diphtheria is endemic in countries all over the world: at the turn of the century it was still one of the most dreaded of all diseases. Today it is relatively rare: complete protection is now available against it.

Ever since the diphtheria bacillus was first described by Klebs in 1883 and then identified in 1884 as the causative agent of diphtheria by Loffler, it has been the subject of intensive research by the bacteriologist and the doctor alike. There is probably no other bacteriological disease so well documented and none whose study has been more fruitful in the science of immunology as a whole. Not only has the doctor an accurate and easily carried out test for susceptibility available to him, but he has access to two methods of immunisation, one passive, which he may use as a curative measure, and the other active, to use as a preventative.

Active immunisation is directed not against the bacillus but against the toxin which it produces. This exotoxin is one of the most potent poisons known. Fortunately it loses its toxic properties when boiled, treated with formalin, or precipitated with alum, without its antigenic properties being affected. A preparation so treated is called a toxoid and it is used to produce active immunity. A suitable artificial medium is inoculated with the bacillus, the culture is incubated for seven days at 37°C and filtered to remove the bacteria. The potency of the toxin is then determined and the toxoid is prepared by treating the solution with formalin, precipitating with alum, and incubating at 40°C until it loses its toxicity. One inoculation with the toxoid usually confers immunity.

Large-scale commercial preparation of the diphtheria antitoxin from the serum of suitably treated horses has made it generally available for use both in the treatment of cases and also as a protection for contacts: its effectiveness depends upon treatment being received during the first two days of the disease. When treatment is given at this early stage, recovery is almost certain: this contrasts sharply with the previous death rate, often as high as 45%.

The susceptibility of an individual to diphtheria may be ascertained by the use of the Schick test. The test is carried out by injecting a specific amount of toxin into the skin: in the absence of antitoxin a local reddening and swelling occurs; if antitoxin is present this neutralises the toxin: if sufficient antitoxin is present to neutralise all the toxin injected then there is no reaction and the subject may be regarded as immune. The interpretation of the results is not, however, so simple as this may appear: a positive reaction may occur in some cases, due to proteins present in the toxin solution, although antitoxins are in fact present. For this reason controls are necessary, fresh toxin is injected into one arm and heated detoxified solution into the other. There are a number of possible results. A reaction on the test arm *only* must be due to antitoxin; a reaction due to protein will occur on *both* arms. A protein reaction is called a false reaction. A positive reaction appears

Test arm	Control arm	Conclusion
Positive	Negative	Susceptible
Negative	Negative	Immune
Positive	False i.e. positive reaction disappears after a few hours	Susceptible (and sensitive to protein)
False	False	Immune (but sensitive to protein)

TABLE 8.

after twenty-four hours and increases for four days while a false reaction reaches full development in twenty-four hours and then fades.

The Schick test applied to a newborn baby shows that a baby is immune as a result of congenital passive immunity if the mother is immune. This immunity is lost by the age of six to twelve months. The percentage of susceptible individuals decreases with age until, by the age of twenty years, 90% are immune. This immunity must be due largely to repeated exposure to the bacillus, which is widespread because of the large number of carriers in the population. The validity of the test as a measure of susceptibility is borne out by investigation into the age incidence of the disease in an unimmunised community which exactly parallels that of susceptibility.

Age	% susceptible
Under 3 months	15
3 to 6 months	30
6 to 12 months	60
1 to 2 years	70
2 to 3 years	60
3 to 4 years	40
4 to 10 years	30
10 to 20 years	20
Over 20 years	12

TABLE 9. Results of Schick test

The Schick test is useful to ascertain whether or not immunisation is necessary, to test whether or not it has been successful, and to help in the diagnosis of doubtful cases.

The incidence of diphtheria carriers in the population is apparently relatively high: probably 0·5 to 1% of the general population harbour the bacillus, while among schoolchildren the rate may be as high as 5%. Immunisation, which is against the toxin and not the organism, does not decrease the percentage of carriers; their continued existence underlines the need for immunisation.

The control of pulmonary tuberculosis

Pulmonary tuberculosis, which is primarily a 'white man's disease', is an ancient complaint and one of the commonest communicable infections of man. There are probably at least 50 million cases in the world today, and it has been spread by the white man to every corner of the globe. In this country its incidence rose sharply during the Industrial Revolution and it was common in England in the nineteenth century when it is estimated that 50% of the population suffered from the disease. Mortality was highest among young men and women: John Keats, Robert Louis Stevenson, Anne, Charlotte, and Emily Bronte were some of its better known victims. Pulmonary tuberculosis is still with us. Routine mass radiography in 1960 revealed that one adult in every 625 required treatment or observation: that is over 70,000 in the adult population as a whole. Anyone may come in contact with one of these open cases – danger is greatest in over-crowded places: factories, cinemas, trains, buses, and shops. Most young people today leave school without having built up an immunity by repeated contacts: the young adult entering industry is therefore in the greatest danger.

There are many different facets to the problem of the control of pulmonary tuberculosis. Improved industrial conditions and better standards of housing and nutrition are of vital importance: these general measures alone would probably do much to reduce its incidence. Equally important are specific measures: early detection of new cases by mass radiography with a vigorous follow-up, the provision of special workshops for tuberculous patients as is provided by Remploy in Birmingham, the placing of recovered patients in suitable jobs and, possibly the most important of all, immunisation with BCG for all school leavers and those whose daily life exposes them to special risk. BCG (Bacillus-Calmette-Guerin) is a vaccine composed of living attenuated tubercle bacilli: it confers lasting immunity on the person inoculated with it. The susceptibility of an individual to tuberculosis may be determined by the tuberculin test (see also Chapter V). There are several methods of applying the test: in the Mantoux test tuberculin is injected into the skin; the Von Pinguet test consists of scratching the skin through a drop of tuberculin, while in the Valmer patch test a strip of sticking plaster impregnated with tuberculin is stuck onto the chest wall. All individuals with a negative result are then inoculated with BCG vaccine. Tuberculosis *can* be eradicated by intensive preventive measures: the problem is now largely economic.

Chemotherapy

The use of antitoxic sera to modify the course of a disease has, as yet, very limited application: much more widespread is the practice of chemotherapy, the use of drugs to attack the germs within the body. Little headway has yet been made in attacking viruses in this way but two groups of compounds, the sulphonamides and the antibiotics have proved to be of incalculable value in the treatment of bacterial infections.

The sulphonamides. The sulphonamides are a large group of closely related chemical compounds. They were first used as drugs in 1935, when Domagk demonstrated the therapeutic value of the red dye prontosil in streptococcal infections. The active agent of prontosil was found to be the sulphonamide, sulphanilamide. Sulphanilamide was the first sulphonamide drug to be extensively used and it proved to be very effective but against only a limited range of bacteria including streptococci, the gonococcus, and the meningococcus. Attempts were therefore made to modify the sulphonamide molecule to produce new sulphonamides with an extended range of activity: some 1,000 such compounds have been made and tested; all but a few proved to be either too toxic or too inactive. One of the earliest discoveries of practical value was sulphapyridine (M. and B. 693), first used in 1938. It had the same range of activity as sulphanilamide but was more powerful and was also effective against the pneumococcus and the dysentery bacilli. Unfortunately it proved to be somewhat toxic and is now rarely used. Sulphathiazole (M. and B. 760) and sulphadiazole are both effective against a wide range of organisms, streptococci, pneumococci, staphylococci, meningococci, and the dysentery bacilli. Neither is markedly toxic, the latter even less so than the former. Sulphaguanidine, which is absorbed very slowly from the alimentary canal, is very useful in bacterial infections of the intestine: it is extensively used in pre- and post-colon surgery. No sulphonamide has any effect against viruses.

All sulphonamides may be administered orally. The majority are excreted quickly; it is therefore important that the drug is taken regularly and that the treatment is continued for the full prescribed period.

Antibiotics. Antibiotics are substances obtained from living moulds. They are powerful drugs, effective against a wide range of bacteria. Penicillin, the first discovered, is probably the best. Its use in medicine dates back only to 1940 though the destructive effect of the mould Penicillium notatum upon staphylococci was observed in 1929 by Sir Alexander Fleming at St Mary's Hospital, London (Plate 8). The active substance in the mould was named penicillin but little interest was shown in it until 1937 when Florey, Chain, and Heatley resumed its study in Oxford, and obtained it in sufficient quantity for it to be tested as an antibacterial drug. The results were dramatic, its potentialities in a world at war were tremendous. The need for large quantities of the drug was urgent and owing to the pressure of the war the preparation could not be undertaken in this country. All relevant information and material was therefore sent to America where research into methods of purification and production of the drug in large quantities was continued with outstanding success. Now the drug is prepared extensively by pharmaceutical houses in this country and its name has become a household word.

Penicillin is now prepared from the mould Penicillium chrysogenum: although its chemical structure is known, its synthesis in the laboratory is not a practical proposition. It is non-toxic[1] and is effective against a wide range of deadly diseases: most staphylococcal and streptococcal infections, pneumonia, gonorrhoea and syphilis, respond very favourably to its administration. It has, however, no effect on the bacteria causing whooping cough, tuberculosis, or on viruses.

The antibiotic used in the treatment of all forms of tuberculosis is streptomycin, produced by the mould Streptomyces griseus: it is especially effective in the early stages of the disease. It is more toxic than penicillin: in its original form it occasionally caused damage to the ear, resulting in deafness and difficulty in balancing but with recent purer products serious symptoms are rare. Chloromycetin is particularly effective in the treatment of typhoid fever and of infantile gastro-enteritis; aureomycin and terramycin are both useful when penicillin and streptomycin fail; erythromycin is used against staphylococcal infections which do not respond to other antibiotics.

---

1. Some individuals develop allergies to penicillin and other antibiotics (see page 100).

Mode of action of sulphonamides and antibiotics

Neither sulphonamide drugs nor antibiotics actually kill the bacteria which they attack: they arrest their growth and reproduction and the bacteria are then destroyed by the natural defences of the body. The mode of action of both types of drug is essentially similar: they interfere with some metabolic activity of the bacterial cell to such an extent that its growth is prevented. This activity cannot be one of the basic processes common to all cells otherwise the drug would damage the cells of the patient's body; it must be some more specialised activity peculiar to the particular type of bacterium against which the drug is effective. If this is so, it explains why the drugs are so highly specific. Each drug can interfere with one type of specialised activity only, this activity may be peculiar to one type of bacterium or restricted to a limited number of kinds, and it is against these bacteria only that the drug is effective.

It is thought that the drugs exert their influence by 'blocking' specific bacterial enzyme systems. The enzymes concerned are engaged in the synthesis from raw materials obtained from the medium in which they live of products essential to the bacterium. The drugs are thought to resemble closely certain of these vital raw materials. They are then accepted by the enzymes instead of these raw materials but cannot be incorporated into the products vital to the bacterium whose construction the enzyme normally promotes. The enzymes are in this way rendered inactive, the bacteria fail to thrive and reproduce and are effectively destroyed by the body's normal defences.

The evolution of resistant strains of bacteria

Experience has shown that after a period of repeated contact between penicillin and a particular type of bacterium, a penicillin-resistant strain of the bacterium may evolve. It has been found, for example, that while the staphylococci in the nasal passages of 'normal' individuals are penicillin-sensitive, the nasal swabs of 50% of hospital nurses contain almost exclusively penicillin-resistant strains. Bacteria mutate very readily; presumably such mutation results in organisms in which the particular metabolic activity interrupted by the penicillin has been replaced by one upon which it has no effect; alternatively both forms may have been present at the beginning of the exposure to penicillin. In a penicillin-rich environment such a mutation is of great survival value to its possessor and natural selection acts in favour of its perpetuation. Fortunately neither the original nor the mutant form of the nasal staphylococci are pathogenic; if they were then a new form of disease resistant to treatment with penicillin would have evolved. The danger of producing disease-causing, penicillin-resistant strains of bacteria by the use of antibiotics is very real and is one of the chief arguments against the general widespread use of penicillin for prophylactic purposes. Those who suck penicillin lozenges as a protection against a current throat infection may be exposing themselves to an even greater danger.

The prophylactic use of antibiotics under strict supervision is on the other hand often very valuable. Streptomycin administered to a tubercular patient before lung surgery is undertaken, prevents spread of bacteria from the damaged lung during the operation. Penicillin given to a patient with rheumatic heart disease before tooth extraction minimises the risk that the streptococci associated with the infected tooth will reach the damaged heart valves which are particularly susceptible to their attack. The important point in the prophylactic use of antibiotics is that the drugs should be given for a specific purpose only and at a specific time.

The use of penicillin in the treatment of treponematoses

Penicillin is effective against all forms of treponematoses. It is essential that the concentration of penicillin in the blood is maintained for a period long enough to kill all treponemes: the introduction of PAM (procaine penicillin G in oil with aluminium monostearate) has made it possible to maintain this concentration with a few intramuscular injections. It is possible that other products may prove even more effective: many are being tested under the auspices of W.H.O. Whether or not PAM remains the most efficacious preparation, one thing is clear – the availability of penicillin remains the key to treponematosis control. The world supply of penicillin may now be great enough to meet the demands for it but in many countries the supply available is still below the level of medical necessity. An essential part of international aid is to ensure the provision of an adequate penicillin supply for treponematosis control in all underdeveloped areas (Plate 9).

CHAPTER IV

The Biological Basis of Immunity

The antigen–antibody reaction

The ability of human tissues to form antibodies is not confined to the reaction against germs. It is a widespread and puzzling phenomenon which is as yet not fully understood. It is, however, of great importance and will now be considered in some detail. When a foreign protein of any type enters the tissues of the body it promotes a reaction. Whether the protein which provokes the reaction is harmless or toxic is of no importance; the response is always similar: the body reacts by producing a specific substance. It is this substance which is antibody and the foreign protein which stimulates its formation is called antigen. Many substances act as antigens, some more effectively than others, but the majority are proteins. White of egg, the surfaces of living micro-organisms, bacterial toxins, other poisons such as snake venom, each results in the production of a specific antibody and usually if the protein is harmful this renders it harmless and makes phagocytosis possible. It cannot be stressed too strongly that each antigen results in the production of its own particular antibody: measles antibody has no effect upon the virus of chickenpox, diphtheria antitoxin is totally ineffective against snake venom.

The antibody is not a new substance but a modified form of an existing one, the gamma globulin of the blood. The modification is an alteration of part of the surface of the gamma globulin molecule, and the modification is such that the modified patch exactly fits some point on the surface of the antigen which promoted its production, so that antigen and antibody stick together. Eventually the antigen becomes completely coated with antibody so that the irritating substance is smothered with one which is harmless. The antigen with its coating of antibody is now no longer resistant to the phagocytes and is engulfed. Gamma globulin molecules are very large and their surfaces may be modified in a large number of different ways. Each antigen induces a modification to fit its own particular pattern and this pattern alone: the antigen–antibody relationship is highly specific. Many particles of a particular antigen may be held together in clumps by their smothering antibody, a process called agglutination: this further facilitates phagocytosis.

The surfaces of micro-organisms are composed of complex organic compounds and contain powerful antigens. Specific antibodies are formed by the body in response to their presence. Coating with antibody renders virulent bacteria harmless and they are then removed by phagocytosis. The position with regard to the viruses is less fully understood: the antibody must meet the virus outside the cell and render it incapable of entering a fresh cell and multiplying within it.

Antibodies are proteins and the problem of their formation is therefore essentially one of the protein synthesis. At least two processes are involved in the synthesis of a protein molecule (see Vol. I). First the polypeptide chain is built up from amino acid residues, then this chain is folded into the form characteristic of the particular protein molecule. It is this second process that is involved in the production of antibody: the polypeptide chain, which, in the absence of antigen, is folded to form a gamma globulin molecule, is, in its presence, folded in a different way to produce a specific antibody.

It is now generally agreed that in the formation of tissue proteins both processes are genetically determined (see Vol. I), but there is considerable disagreement about the role of the genes in controlling the second process during antibody formation. There are at present two contrasting hypotheses. The first theory contends that it is not the genes but the antigens which control the second process, the folding of the polypeptide chain: its final form is determined from 'without' rather than from 'within'. The theory is therefore called the instructive theory. The plastic polypeptide chain is, when in contact with the antigen, folded into a specific pattern which is then stabilised by the formation of sulphide and hydrogen bonds. As soon as stability is achieved the antigen is set free to act again in the same way. The whole process takes place within the antibody-producing cells. Attractive as this theory is, it does not explain how the body distinguishes between self and non-self or how the 'education' of cells in antibody production is achieved.

In contrast to the instructive theory, the selective theory contends that both stages of the process of antibody formation are genetically controlled: different cells have an inherited ability to produce specific types of antibodies and all that contact with the antigen does is 'trigger off' their production. The antibody forming cells are derived from the mesenchyme of the embryo (see Vol. I): the descendants of the different mesenchyme cells produce groups of antibody forming cells in the adult body. It is suggested that the cells of each such group are concerned with the production of one specific antibody, the ability being gene controlled and the genetic differences having arisen by somatic mutation of the original mesenchyme cells. It is estimated that in this way there have probably come into being at least 10,000 different types of antibody producing cells each capable of turning out a particular antibody. Unlike the instructive theory, the selective theory provides some answer to the two vital questions mentioned above. The problem of the handing on of information to succeeding generations of antibody producing cells does not arise: the information is already there, built into the gene complex. An explanation of the ability to distinguish between self and non-self is a little more difficult: the following suggestion has been made. Potential antibody forming cells in the embryo are actually destroyed by contact with antigens: during embryonic life the various self-proteins will come into contact with the groups of cells which form antibodies against them and these cells will be destroyed. By the time it is born, the baby has therefore lost for good the capacity to form antibodies against its own tissues. It is estimated that by this time about half of the groups of antibody producing cells have been destroyed; the 5,000 which remain are capable of producing antibodies in response to some 5,000 foreign antigens which may be contacted post-natally.

Interferon

Although it is certain that immunity to virus diseases is due to antibodies, it has long been doubted if they are responsible for recovery from a first attack. There exist certain individuals who, for some little understood reason, are unable to form antibodies; although in the days before the use of antibiotics became general, any bacterial infection would (to these individuals) have proved fatal, virus infections followed their normal course, often ending in recovery.

It has now been discovered that a cell invaded by viruses produces a chemical substance, interferon, which blocks virus reproduction. This substance was first discovered during the study of the phenomenon of virus interference, the way in which the invasion of the tissues by one virus may protect them from invasion by another: when one virus invades a group of cells a second virus is prevented from doing so. This may explain why, for example, paralytic poliomyelitis is more prevalent in countries with a high level of public health and sanitation and rare in those where the standard is low. In the latter countries the susceptible cells are invaded by some common intestinal virus which causes viral interference and keeps the poliomyelitis virus out. Where health standards are higher the intestinal viruses do not enter the cells which are therefore wide open to invasion by poliomyelitis.

The substance which promotes the formation of interferon is the nucleic acid of the virus: indeed, experimental evidence shows that its production is the cell's response to its invasion by any type of nucleic acid. Like antibody, interferon is a protein, but it differs from antibody in that it is non-specific: interferon produced in response to cell invasion by one type of virus is effective in blocking multiplication of any other. The interferons produced by various animal species differ slightly one from another, and although that produced by animals of any one species is more effective in protecting animals of that species, nevertheless it affords some protection when introduced into the cells of animals of any other. Neither does an animal produce antibodies against 'foreign' interferon: the degree of similarity must be such that the protein of the interferon is not recognised as 'foreign'.

Interferon does not prevent the entry of the virus into the cell but blocks its reproduction. In some way the interferon produced in response to the presence in the cell of the 'foreign' nucleic acid inhibits the replication of that nucleic acid; exactly how is not known.

It is highly probable that the virulence of any particular virus is closely linked to its relationship to interferon. There are two possibilities. It may be that the amount of interferon produced depends upon the nature of the invading virus. Recent work shows that in some cases at least, the virulence of the virus fluctuates inversely with the amount of interferon produced: the more virulent the virus, the less interferon there is produced as the result of its presence in the cell. Or, to put it the other way round, the amount of interferon which is produced as a result of its presence determines the virulence of a virus. Alternatively, as other experimental work indicates, the virulence of a virus may be determined not by the amount of interferon present but by the susceptibility of that virus to it: the more sensitive the virus, the less virulent it will be.

It is probable that the interferon mechanism was originally evolved to preserve the integrity of the genetic structure of cells, by protecting them from foreign nucleic acids in general, and its production following virus invasion of a cell is a fortuitous chance. This is a chance of which man may learn to take full advantage. Interferon appears in many ways to be an ideal anti-viral agent in man. It is non-specific and acts on a wide range of viruses, it is non-toxic and, as it does not induce antibody formation, it may be used frequently without loss of effect. Two possibilities suggest themselves, reminiscent of the passive and active immunities produced by immunisation: the production of interferon on a commercial scale in the tissues of other animals or the development of 'foreign' interferon which, when injected into his tissues, will stimulate the individual to produce his own interferon. As with antibodies in immunology, the latter method, like the use of vaccines to stimulate antibody production, may prove more efficient than the former which has its parallel in the direct administration of ready-made antibody.

Other important antigen–antibody reactions

Sensitisation. So far consideration has been given only to those antibodies which enter the circulation and remain free in the blood. It is now known that some antibodies are removed from the blood and incorporated in the cells of various tissues. These antibodies are then said to be fixed and the tissues of the individual are said to be sensitised to the particular antigen. The fixed antibodies remain in the cells long after the first invasion of the antigen and perhaps permanently. When the antigen enters the body again and comes into contact with the fixed antibody, a strong reaction takes place between them as a result of which typical inflammatory reactions take place in the immediate neighbourhood.

Tuberculin test for tuberculosis. The fact that inflammation occurs wherever antigen reacts with a fixed antibody has a number of practical applications: one of the best known is the tuberculin test for tuberculosis. If a child has been infected with tuberculosis or has been immunised against it then antibodies formed against the tubercle bacillus will have become fixed in the cells, including those of the skin. If a little tuberculin, a substance prepared from the bacillus which, though harmless, has the antigenic properties of the living germ, is scratched into the skin, then after forty-eight hours the scratched area is seen to be inflamed: the tuberculin has reacted with the fixed antibody and histamine has been released. In this way large numbers of children can be tested for their susceptibility to tuberculosis prior to immunisation with BCG vaccine: a positive result – inflammation – indicates immunity or active tuberculosis, which would be checked by X-ray; a negative one – absence of inflammation – means susceptibility.

Allergies. Although the presence of fixed antibodies in the cells can in some cases be put to a useful purpose, in others it may have unpleasant or even disastrous consequences. Some unfortunate individuals appear to have an inherited tendency to produce antibodies against substances which do not similarly affect others: these antibodies are of a specialised type called reagens. As these antibodies become very firmly fixed in the cells, a state of heightened sensitivity is developed which is known as an allergy. In the sensitised individual, contact with the offending antigen produces the characteristic symptoms of some specific allergic disease.

One such condition is serum sickness which, in the susceptible individual, follows a second injection of an antitoxic serum such as that used to give protection against tetanus or diphtheria. Such sera are solutions containing horse protein, modified, it is true, to form antitoxin but nevertheless horse, and therefore 'foreign' protein. The susceptible individual, on receiving the first injection of serum, forms antibodies against this protein and these become fixed in the cells all over the body. The antigen present in the second injection then reacts with this fixed antibody and histamine is released, perhaps locally producing little more than an itchy rash, perhaps generally leading to widespread severe symptoms and even to complete collapse. A few individuals react in a similar way to antibiotics like penicillin.

Two of the best known allergic conditions, which are also two of the most distressing because it is rarely possible to avoid contact with the causal antigens, are hay fever and asthma. The antigens which cause hay fever are usually contained in the pollen grains of various plants, especially the grasses. As pollen-laden dust is breathed in through the nose, grains are absorbed by the lining membrane and their absorption is followed, in susceptible individuals, by the production of antibody. This antibody then becomes fixed in cells all over the body, including those of the membranes lining the nose and covering the eyes. Antibody fixed at these two sites is very likely to make renewed contact with antigen: when this happens histamine is released and the result is the distressing swollen, red, watering condition of the nose and eyes typical of an attack of hay fever. The condition can often be relieved by the use of anti-histamine drugs.

An attack of asthma, characterised by a paroxysm of extremely difficult breathing, is brought about by the constriction of the bronchioles by the contraction of the muscles in their walls accompanied by swelling of their lining membrane. In the asthmatic subject, the cells of this lining membrane have become sensitised to some specific antigen: two of the commonest offenders are the dust from feathers and the orris root in face powder. Histamine is released when the antigen reacts with the fixed antibody in the sensitised cells in the bronchioles and causes not only the swelling of the lining, but also constriction of the bronchioles because the muscles of the bronchioles are particularly susceptible to its effects.[1]

The reactions causing hay fever take place in the nose and eyes and those causing asthma in the lungs because it is with antibody fixed in cells in these regions that the antigen comes into contact. But the antibody is also fixed in many other cells, probably all over the body and certainly in the skin. Use is made of this skin sensitisation in identifying the antigen to

---

1. The symptoms of asthma are not always due to allergy: attacks may also follow lung infection or damage or be instigated by some psychological disturbance.

which the patient is susceptible: when a solution containing this antigen is placed on a scratch made in the skin the signs of inflammation appear as the antigen reacts with the fixed antibody. Solutions of various possible antigens may be tested in this way and the one responsible identified. In fortunate cases the antigen is one with which the patient can in future avoid contact.

Some individuals may develop food allergies when they become sensitised to substances present in certain foods, especially eggs and shellfish: gastro-intestinal upsets follow when the offending foods are eaten. Sensitisation of the skin cells of susceptible babies often to antigens present in the mother's milk leads to the condition of infantile eczema, a distressing complaint which usually clears up by the age of eighteen months.

It is noticed that frequently several members of the same family show allergic reactions of different types or that any one individual has more than one allergic tendency. This is because it is the tendency to become sensitised, rather than to develop a specific allergy, which is inherited.

Other antigen–antibody reactions

It has already been indicated that many substances foreign to the body of a particular individual are antigenic when introduced into it, and provoke the formation of antibodies. In addition to the extrinsic substances already described which may accidently enter the tissues, antigenic substances have been shown to be present in many of the body's own tissues so that, if such tissues are transferred from one individual to another, undesirable consequences may result. Important in this connection are the antigens in the blood – upon whose occurrence the classification of the population into different blood groups is based – and those present in the skin. The former are of great significance in blood transfusions; the latter put severe limitations on the operation of skin grafting and organ transplantation.

Blood grouping antigens. The blood of human beings may be classified in a number of different ways depending on the presence or absence in it of certain antigens. A large number of groups and sub-groups of these antigens have already been identified and more are still being discovered: it may eventually be found that so many different combinations are possible that no two individuals are exactly alike, and the time may even come when determination of blood grouping rivals comparison of fingerprints as a means of identification.

Rhesus grouping. The red blood cells of some 85% of the individuals in this country contain on their surfaces a chemical substance known as the Rhesus factor, so called because it was first identified in the red blood cells of the Rhesus monkey. If blood of this type is introduced into the body of an individual whose red blood cells do not contain this factor, then the factor acts as an antigen and antibodies are formed which coat the transfused corpuscles and cause them to stick together in clumps, a process which is known as agglutination. The 85% of the population who possess the factor are said to be Rhesus positive (Rh+); the 15% who do not are Rhesus negative (Rh−).

Compatibility of Rhesus group is essential in blood transfusions. The antigen is a powerful one, and if Rh+ blood is introduced into the body of an Rh− individual, this individual will produce antibodies which will agglutinate the transfused corpuscles. Although the first transfusion is not likely to be dangerous, the effect, as in the development of immunity, is cumulative and a second transfusion may have serious consequences for the recipient.

A difference in Rhesus grouping between mother and foetus may cause danger to the unborn baby. The foetal and maternal circulations are separated in the placenta only by a very thin membrane and although this does not normally allow blood to pass through there may in some instances be a leakage allowing foetal blood to pass into the mother. If the mother is Rh− and the foetus Rh+ (this may happen when the father is Rh+, see Vol. I), then the foetal blood entering the maternal circulation provokes the formation of antibodies. These antibodies pass back into the foetus. The baby is thus in the extremely unhappy position of agglutinating his own red blood cells.

A baby who is affected in this way may be born with haemolytic disease. The affected baby is anaemic and jaundiced: the jaundice is due to the inability of the liver to deal with the excess of bilirubin formed by the breakdown of haemoglobin which, circulating in the blood, causes the characteristic yellow colour. If the condition is only slight, the baby, freed from its supply of maternal antibodies will recover unaided; severely affected babies, however, need immediate treatment to save their lives. The treatment takes the form of a blood transfusion: the transfused blood must be Rh−; only blood of this group is unaffected by antibodies present in the baby's blood. In very serious cases an exchange transfusion may be necessary; small quantities of blood are alternately withdrawn and replaced by fresh blood via the umbilical vein until 90% of the blood has been changed: the lives of a very high percentage of affected babies are now saved in this way.

The baby will in time destroy the antibodies in his circulation; his own blood will then cease to be agglutinated and most babies make a complete recovery.

The chance of a Rh− woman marrying a Rh+ man is about six to one. Such marriages give either a 100% certainty or a 50:50 chance (see Vol. I) of the foetus being Rh+. Yet only about one such pregnancy in forty has any complications. There are several reasons for this. The placenta may not leak and so no antibodies are formed. Even if the placenta does leak antibodies are not likely to be produced in large quantities during the first pregnancy: a first child does not usually show any symptoms. It is only in later pregnancies that children are likely to be seriously affected. Modern techniques now make it possible to desensitise the mother by the injection of anti-Rhesus serum immediately after the birth of the first baby so that the risk to the second and subsequent babies is reduced to a minimum.

If the mother is Rhesus positive and the foetus Rhesus negative no symptoms will develop, even if the placenta leaks, because foetal tissue does not form antibodies.

ABO blood grouping

In this classification there are four main groups to one of which every human being belongs: these groups are A, B, AB, and O. The grouping is based upon the presence or absence in the blood of four chemical substances, two contained on the surfaces of the red blood corpuscles and two in the plasma, which, on account of their behaviour are known as antigens and antibodies respectively. It must be stressed, however, that the antibodies are not, like those previously described, formed as a result of the invasion of the tissues by an antigen: they are naturally present in the blood of people belonging to certain groups. The two antigens, which are called A and B, may be present singly or together, or both may be absent: the individuals, then, belong to group A, B, AB, or O respectively. The antibodies present in the serum are called anti-A and anti-B: these antibodies will cause agglutination of corpuscles containing the A and B antigens respectively. A and anti-A, B and anti-B, therefore, never occur together in the same blood, but if A is absent, anti-B is present, while B and anti-A always occur together. The antigen-antibody distribution is therefore as shown in Table 10.

Group	Antigens	Antibodies
A	A	Anti-B
B	B	Anti-A
AB	A and B	Neither
O	Neither	Anti-A and anti-B

TABLE 10.

If bloods are mixed red blood corpuscles containing antigen A are agglutinated by plasma containing anti-A; those containing B by plasma containing anti-B. This phenomenon is of vital importance in blood transfusions: incompatible antigens and antibodies should not normally be brought together. If whole blood is transfused agglutination is avoided with certainty only if blood of the same group is given, and if large quantities of blood are required this is essential. However, in an emergency, provided no more than one pint of blood is given, the antibodies in the donor's plasma are so diluted in the recipient's circulation that their effects can be discounted. Only the effects of the donor's antigens on the recipient's antibodies therefore need be taken into account. Individuals belonging to group O, having no antigens, are universal donors.

Recipient	Donors
A	A, O
B	B, O
AB	A, B, AB, O
O	O

TABLE 11.

Determination of the ABO blood group is a relatively simple matter. If blood from an individual belonging to group A is allowed to clot, the serum which can be collected contains the anti-B antibody; the serum from a group B individual contains anti-A. This serum is then concentrated and can be stored for years in a deep freeze. Two drops of the blood to be grouped are placed on a microscope slide and anti-A serum is added to the first drop and anti-B to the second. After one to three minutes, one of the four following results will be obtained.

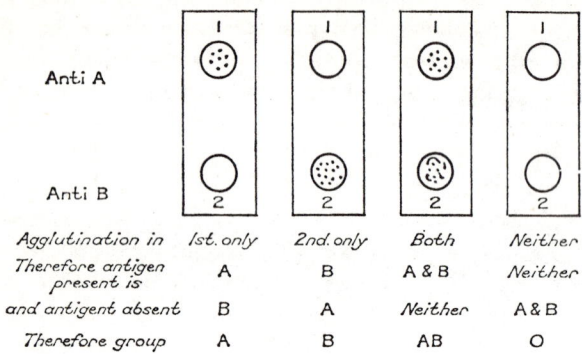

FIG. 8. Identifying the ABO blood groups.

The chemistry of the blood group antigens

The blood grouping antigens are very difficult to remove from the surfaces of the corpuscles and are not easily obtained in pure form in sufficient quantity for analysis. Recently, however, it has been discovered that the antigens are not confined to the red blood cells but that they are also present in the mucous secretions from other cells of the body. They are now obtained in sufficiently large quantities for extensive study from saliva, gastric juice, the meconium evacuated from the alimentary canal of the new-born baby, and from the accumulation of mucous secretion which forms certain types of cysts. The antigens have proved on analysis to be mucoproteins. The mucoprotein consists of a protein backbone to which are attached a number of chain-like polysaccharides (see Vol. I). Each polysaccharide chain itself consists of a number of component chains: each link of these chains is a ring-like sugar molecule of which several different types are present. Recent investigation has shown that it is the polysaccharides and not the proteins which act as antigens, the antibodies reacting with the ends of the polysaccharide chains. It is differences between the sugars which form the ends of the chains which give the antigens their specificity. The number of sugar rings involved in 'fitting' the antibody varies from two to six. Presumably the difference between one blood group antigen and another is in the number and nature of the significant sugar molecules. In the B blood group it is the last two sugars of each chain, which are the antigen. In the A group the polysaccharide chain presumably has a different type of ending, while in the AB group the two types are probably attached alternately along the length of the protein chain. It is interesting to relate this knowledge of antigen structure to what is known of gene action: presumably specific genes are responsible for adding particular sugars to the ends of the polysaccharide chains: one gene adds sugars to produce the A antigen, its allele adds sugars which give the B, while in individuals of the AB group both genes are present and polysaccharide chains of both types are formed (see Vol. I).

Antigens and skin-grafting

It has now been shown that antigens are also present in other tissues of the body, though it is still uncertain whether they are identical with those in the fluids and on the red blood cells. These antigens become important when skin grafting or organ transplantation is to be undertaken. When attempts are made to graft skin from one individual to another, with the possible exception of identical twins or closely related members of the same family, the graft frequently fails to 'take' and the operation is unsuccessful. The skin-donor's antigens have provoked the recipient to produce antibodies which have reacted with the cells of the graft and prevented it from 'taking'. One notable exception is the cornea: as this is avascular, it can be successfully grafted from one individual to another.

Considerable advances have been made in the last few years in kidney – and more recently in heart – transplantation. The success of such operations depends upon careful tissue typing to ensure that the transplanted organs will be reasonably acceptable to the recipient, and upon the treatment of the recipient before and, should it be necessary, after surgery with immuno-suppressive drugs which control rejection. The use of such drugs is dangerous. The patient, unprotected by normal antibody formation, is wide open to infection and also runs the risk of severe internal bleeding.

Kidney grafting is now undertaken with some success: the feasibility of heart transplantation is still doubtful – to date only two transplanted hearts are still beating in the bodies of their new owners.

CHAPTER V

Environmental Hazards to Health

It is now clear that as medical science continues to advance, disease-causing organisms will cease to be the most serious of the hazards to health: in many parts of the world today man no longer lives in constant fear of death from infection. But as we take our children to be immunised and send our milk to be pasteurised and a new-found confidence replaces the old terror, the seeds of new hazards are germinating in our environment – seeds which we ourselves have sown in our world as part of the price of progress. As a result, the air we breathe, the earth we live on, and its rivers and seas are becoming contaminated with ever more dangerous materials, the inevitable by-products of man's constant struggle to control and exploit the environment in which he lives.

Some of these contaminants are natural products which have been a part of the background ever since man walked the earth, but others are new substances altogether, substances which man has himself created by his own alchemy. We do not yet understand fully how serious pollution of the environment by these substances may turn out to be.

Smog

For four days in December 1952, Londoners were dying at the rate of over 1,000 per day, a death rate comparable with the worst days of the great plague epidemics of the sixteenth and seventeenth centuries. But this time the cause was man-made: the worst type of atmospheric pollution – smog. Smog occurs in areas where fog is associated with the smoke which comes from burning coal. Fog occurs when there is a sudden cooling of moisture-laden air without any wind to blow it away: in clean air the water forms little clear droplets; in dirty air it condenses round the sooty particles and the result is smog.

Burning coal adds three types of pollution to the atmosphere: smoke which consists of soot and tarry material; grit; and the gas sulphur dioxide, which is also produced by the burning of fuel oil. The main danger to man seems to come from the association of sulphur dioxide with smoke: sulphur dioxide alone does not usually appear to be harmful.

There is ever-increasing evidence that the continual inhalation of polluted air is associated with various types of respiratory complaints: important among these are chronic bronchitis and, probably, lung cancer.

Chronic bronchitis is a distressing disease, the most obvious symptoms of which are breathlessness on exertion and a wheezy cough. The disease is incapacitating and has a high death rate – over 37,000 in England and Wales in 1961. The death rate shows a marked regional difference, high rates being associated with the dirty atmosphere of the industrial cities: there is a marked difference in incidence between the counties lying North and South of a line drawn from the mouth of the river Severn to the Wash. In England and Wales the death rate is one hundred times greater than in Norway. Smog aggravates chronic bronchitis, especially in the elderly among whom the condition is most common, and it was among this age group that the high death rate occurred in December 1952.

The incidence of lung cancer is on the increase, the number of deaths from this cause having risen from nine per million in 1900 to 370 per million in 1954. It is now a major killing disease in this country: it claimed 6,568 victims in 1944, 17,271 in 1955 and over 22,000 in 1960. The death rate from pulmonary tuberculosis in that year was 3,108. The disease is more common in this country than anywhere else in the world, and as with chronic bronchitis, the death rate is greater in towns than in rural areas, suggesting that once again polluted atmosphere may be a contributory factor.

Dust

By virtue of the nature of their daily occupation many thousands of workers in this country and elsewhere breathe air heavily contaminated with dust. Dust is defined as particles or aggregates of particles measuring from 150 microns to 0·5 microns in diameter which are suspended in the air. Although a seemingly harmless substance, dust can nevertheless constitute a grave hazard to health. Some forms when inhaled over long periods of time can be highly dangerous. The small particles, those with a diameter of 5 microns or less, reach the alveoli of the lungs, settle, and, depending on the nature of the particles and the extent of the contamination, cause diseases of varying degrees of severity. These diseases, which are seriously debilitating and frequently fatal, are collectively known as the pneumoconioses.

Silicosis

The damage which the dust does to the lungs appears to be chemical rather than mechanical, so that not all dusts are equally harmful: among the worst offenders are those which contain free silica; the pneumoconiosis caused by prolonged inhalation of silica is known as silicosis. In its early stages silicosis is a mild condition involving only slight difficulty in breathing on exertion. As the disease progresses, this difficulty becomes more severe and the patient develops a persistent cough: at this stage working capacity begins to be reduced. Finally the disease leads to total incapacity and death from heart failure usually follows.

Silicosis has a world-wide distribution. It is associated with industries which involve the production of large quantities of dust containing free silica, usually in the form of quartz. These industries include the sandstone and granite industries, the pottery industry, coal mining, slate quarrying, and the iron and steel industries.

The quarrying and working of sandstone are probably the most widespread of the silicosis-producing industries in Britain today. Sandstone is extensively quarried in many areas in North, Central, and South-west England and has been used in the construction of many famous buildings: the beautiful Anglican cathedral in Liverpool is being built from a lovely locally-quarried rock and the material for the building of nineteenth century Edinburgh came from sandstone quarries now exhausted. Sandstone is a particularly pleasing building material: the warm brown stone from Yorkshire and the rich red rock from Dumfries are especially lovely. Unfortunately sandstones are siliceous: sedimentary rocks consisting very largely of quartz grains held together by cementing material with a free silica content as high as 75 to 95%. Some 32,000 men are involved in some branch of the sandstone industry as quarrymen, stone masons, or in one of a variety of other activities. The incidence of silicosis among these workers may be as high as 40%.

Granite is much in demand as a building material and for monumental work. The centre of the industry is the granite city of Aberdeen which replaced the wooden town destroyed by fire in 1741. Much of the granite used in this country now is, however, imported, largely from Scandinavia. Granite is an igneous rock containing up to 30% of free silica. It is very hard which makes it eminently suitable for buildings, for pavements, and for monuments. The dust formed during its working is, fortunately, lower in silica content than sandstone dust and therefore less liable to cause silicosis. Nevertheless, it is by no means a negligible hazard to the health of those exposed to it: in one series of investigations 17% of the workers in the industry showed evidence of silicosis.

Slate is a cleaved rock containing up to 60% free silica in the form of quartz. Blocks of rock are first sawn up in the mills and then split with chisel and mallet into large slates which are finally sawn into the required size. About 10,000 men are employed in the slate quarries of North Wales, and the risk of silicosis is high.

In the five towns of the potteries, now federated in the County Borough of Stoke-on-Trent, live many thousands of workers, over half of whom are engaged in some branch of the pottery industry. In 1720 John Astbury introduced into his pottery to improve its firing qualities, finely powdered flint, a practice which has persisted until this day. Unfortunately flint is the calcidonic form of uncombined silica, a potential cause of silicosis.

In the manufacture of earthenware the ingredients—which include china clay and powdered flint—are mixed into a firm, moist paste which is shaped into various articles. The partially dried article is then smoothed on a revolving disc throwing off fine silica-containing dust which may be inhaled by the potter. Flint is not added to the mixture from which china is made, but the delicate pieces are supported during firing in powdered flint: when this flint is scoured off after removal from the kiln the fine dust contaminates the atmosphere. Furthermore, flint is actually used as an abrasive during the final polishing after decorating and glazing. Again the danger of silicosis is obvious.

The founding of metal is one of the most ancient crafts known. It is a major industry in Britain today: steel foundries employ many thousands of men in Durham, Yorkshire, Lancashire, Cheshire, South Wales, and on the Clyde, and iron foundries in Scotland and the Black Country.

During the founding process the molten metal is poured into moulds. The silica sand which is used in the construction of the moulds contains a very high proportion of free silica. A very high temperature is needed to melt the metal, and at this temperature the molten metal actually penetrates into the sand mould: the sand is then firmly burnt onto the metal casing. This burnt-on sand has then to be removed: however this is done, a certain amount of silica dust is bound to be inhaled by the worker. Although preventive measures have now greatly minimised the risk, the danger of contracting silicosis still exists. The disease has always been more prevalent among steel than among iron workers: while the melting point of iron is 1,100°C that of steel is 1,600°C and at this higher temperature the burning on of the molten metal is more extensive. Also, the sand used in the construction of the steel moulds contains up to 99% silica, while that used for iron moulds has not more than 80% silica and often less.

Over 90% of the recorded cases of silicosis are found among coal miners, especially those who work in the coal mines of South Wales where anthracite mines are particularly dangerous. The dusts which get into the atmosphere come from the shale, sandstone, and other rocks which may contain anything from 40% to 85% free silica.

Prevention of silicosis

Theoretically the prevention of silicosis would appear to be a simple matter: if no silica dust gets into the air which people breathe then there will be no silicosis. Most types of mining and many factory processes are inherently dusty, so that total elimination of silica dust in this way may be an impossibility. Nevertheless there are many practical measures which can be adopted to reduce the risk.

Wherever possible, alternative harmless materials can be substituted for dangerous ones. Limestone can be used as a building stone instead of sandstone or granite: unfortunately limestone is adversely affected by the acid atmosphere of the industrial towns and cities. Alternative materials to the dangerous sandstones can be used for grinding: steel rollers have replaced the sandstone millstones used in the flour industry, wheels of carborundum, emery, or alumina are gradually superseding the sandstone ones so long used in the grinding, sharpening, and polishing of metals. Powdered alumina can be used instead of flint for protecting china in the kiln and for polishing it after firing. The use of sand in blasting operations is now prohibited: alternative materials like steel shot and calcined alumina must be used.

If the production of silica dust is inevitable, then it can often be controlled and kept away from the worker, or failing this, the worker himself can be protected so that he does not inhale the dust. Dust may be removed by various ventilation systems: probably the most effective is an adaptation of the familiar laboratory fume cupboard – exhaust ventilation combined with enclosure of the process. Water, oil, and foam may be used to allay the dust: in hard rock mining, wet drilling is widely used, and the hydroblast – a high velocity jet of sand and water – is proving satisfactory and safe in the cleaning of metal castings. The worker who is forced to operate in a dusty atmosphere should wear either a dust-mask or respirator of some type.

Asbestiosis

Asbestos is a material which is playing an increasingly important part in modern life. It is extensively used in the manufacture of specialised textiles, for brake linings, and in the lagging of pipes and boilers. Asbestos is a mixture of fibrous silicates, especially magnesium silicate.

Workers in the asbestos industry are subject to a specific form of pneumoconiosis known as asbestiosis. This disease, like all other pneumoconioses, is a distressing and debilitating condition and again the best preventative treatment is rigorous dust suppression, supplemented by the use of efficient respiratory equipment.

Pneumoconiosis of coal miners

Coal miners in mines all over the world suffer from chronic pulmonary disease brought about by the inhalation of mixed coal dust containing often only a small proportion of silica. In Britain this form of pneumoconiosis is responsible for more deaths than all other types put together and is the greatest medical and social problem in industry. As in true silicosis, the earliest symptom of the disease is difficulty in breathing but the accompanying coughing produces a coal-black sputum. Bronchitis and tuberculosis are frequent complications. The disease can be totally incapacitating and is often fatal. The essential protective measures, as in true silicosis, are the removal of dust by effective ventilation, the use of water, and the protection of the miners with respirators when other methods are impracticable.

In 1952 the National Coal Board initiated a Pneumoconiosis Field Research scheme to relate the findings of medical examination of miners in twenty-five selected collieries to existing working conditions: this made it possible to establish a safe, permissible level of dustiness. Strenuous efforts were made in South Wales where the situation was most serious and by 1956 the dust level had been reduced to one tenth of its 1942 value. The incidence of pneumoconiosis among the miners fell from 5·56% in 1945 to 0·92% in 1955. In other parts of the country the results have been disappointing: a rise from 0·03% to 0·58% has been recorded. It is obvious that there is still much improvement to be made.

Effects of pneumoconiosis

Apart from the toll of pneumoconiosis in terms of human suffering, the loss to the community in terms of working hours and compensation is enormous. In the coal-mining industry alone, the annual liability is in the region of £2,000,000. Through its ravages the industry loses many skilled workers every year and these highly trained men may themselves experience great difficulty in obtaining alternative employment, adding severe mental anxiety to the existing physical incapacity.

The cotton industry

Raw cotton is spun in the card rooms of the cotton mills. The cotton which enters the card room is dusty: when it leaves the carding engines it is almost dust free. Unless adequate precautions are taken the cotton dust enters the atmosphere of the card room and is inhaled by the operatives. Those who work for long periods in such card rooms develop an allergic type of respiratory disease known as byssinosis. The patient experiences difficulty in breathing, often of an asthmatic type, accompanied by coughing. Although slow in onset, causing no disability for ten years or more, the condition gets progressively worse and may lead in time to total incapacity and even to death.

In good mills every effort is made to reduce the amount of cotton dust in the atmosphere but this is a complex engineering problem. Screening of personnel before employment can be very helpful: no one with a family history of allergic conditions or who is a habitual mouth breather should become a cotton operative. The problem has, however, not yet been solved: many workers, particularly in the more dusty mills, still suffer from byssinosis.

Ionising radiation

Radioactive dust is a comparatively new health hazard but one which is becoming increasingly serious. It is but one aspect of the whole problem of exposure to ionising radiations of all types.

The nature of ionising radiations and their effect as mutagens is considered in Volume I: here the concern is with their effect, not upon future generations, but upon the individual—the unborn infant, the child, and the adult. Detailed investigation has shown conclusively that excessive exposure to radiation results at all ages in damage to tissues: the highly reactive products formed as a result of ionisation result in disastrous changes in both the structure and the metabolism of the cells. Cells are not equally susceptible at all times; damage appears to be greatest in actively dividing cells, especially just before a division begins.

Collection of information about the effects of radiation on human tissues is made difficult by the, mercifully, limited number of cases where some change in the tissues can, without question, be attributed to the effects of radioactivity. The information which is available has come from the study of the case histories of the early medical research workers whose pioneer investigations in the field of radioactivity preceded any appreciation of its danger; from investigation into the fate of people who worked without protection in certain occupations involving radioactivity before the hazards of exposure were understood; from the careful, prolonged follow-up of patients who received radiotherapy for malignant disease; and from the examination of the victims of atomic bomb explosions in Japan in 1945 and near the Marshall Islands in 1947. A considerable amount of experimental work is also carried out with animals: as the effects vary considerably from species to species it cannot be assumed that the results of such experiments are necessarily directly applicable to man.

From all such observations it has been possible to draw a number of important conclusions. The damage varies directly with the nature, intensity, rate, and duration of the exposure: there are certain thresholds below which there is no effect, and when damage is done, some recovery is possible. This is in sharp contrast to the genetic effects where every exposure is potentially dangerous, the effects are cumulative and there is no recovery. The effects also depend upon how much, and which part of, the body is exposed. The most sensitive tissues are those whose cells are actively dividing: lymph glands, the lining of the small intestine, and the blood forming cells of the red bone marrow are particularly sensitive. Least affected are adult nervous and muscular tissue where all cells are mature. Young children are inevitably more susceptible than adults and the unborn baby is the most sensitive of all.

It is important to distinguish between the immediate and the long term effects of excessive exposure to radiation – those which appear within a few weeks of exposure and those which become apparent only after many years. While damage of both types follows exposure to radiation of very high intensity, however brief the duration, it is more than possible that delayed effects may also be produced by radiation of quite low intensity if exposure is sufficiently prolonged. While the former condition is not likely to be met with in normal civilian life, it is possible that the latter may even now comprise a very real risk to at least certain groups of the population, and the danger may become greater and more widespread if the amount of radioactive material in the atmosphere continues to increase.[1]

The immediate effects of intense radiation are seen when either the whole or some part of the body is exposed. Exposure to such intense radiation is fortunately rare: two sources of information are, however, available. In 1945 two atomic bombs

1. Natural and man made sources of radiation are discussed in Vol. I.

were dropped on Hiroshima and Nagasaki in Japan, giving a massive dose of radiation to many of the inhabitants, and in 1947, following the test-firing of a nuclear weapon in the Pacific Ocean, there was heavy radioactive fall-out on one of the Marshall Islands to which the islanders were inevitably exposed. The immediate effect of such exposure is the onset, within a few hours or even minutes, of radiation sickness. Nausea, vomiting, and diarrhoea may be followed by collapse and death. Alternatively, there may be recovery, which appears to be complete, but investigation shows very low red and white blood cell counts and some two to four weeks later the victim again becomes ill. Haemorrhages occur in the skin and mucous membranes, and the hair falls out. Death may follow, often from infection: if recovery takes place it is slow and convalescence is prolonged. All the victims of the Japanese explosions who were subjected to 500 or more röntgens and not killed outright were severely ill, and 50% died: at 100 röntgens sickness was less severe, affecting only 15% of those exposed, all of whom recovered. It is estimated that the Marshall Islanders were exposed to about 170 röntgens; illness was mild, ulcerations and haemorrhages healed completely, and there were no deaths.

Massive doses of radiation may be given to limited parts of the body during radiotherapy: the rest of the body – and that of the radiotherapist – is most carefully protected by a shield through which the radiation cannot penetrate. The immediate effects vary with the intensity of the dosage and the part of the body treated: serious radiation sickness is rare. There may, however, be some reddening and blistering of the skin. The effects are more serious in young children.

Radiation and blood disease

It is now definitely established that exposure to radiation produces delayed effects which may not be fully evident for many years. Investigations have been made into the nature of these effects both after a single brief intense exposure and also after a prolonged period of repeated exposure to smaller doses. The results are apparently similar in both cases and include the development of leukaemia, severe anaemia, and cancer. The method of investigation is to compare the rate of incidence of the condition in groups of people who have been exposed to radiation with the rate in comparable groups of individuals who have not.

The development of leukaemia was extensively studied by the U.S.A. Atomic Bomb Casualty Commission in Japan between 1947 and 1955. The expected number of deaths from leukaemia in an unexposed population the size of Hiroshima and Nagasaki with the same age and sex distribution was estimated at 25: among those inhabitants who had been in the two towns in 1945, at the time of the explosion, and still remained in 1955, there were 91 proven and 14 suspected fatal cases. The relationship between nearness to the centre of the explosion and the incidence was also significant as Table 12 shows.

Distance from centre of explosion in metres	Estimated exposure	Incidence per 10,000 of population Jan. 1947–Aug. 1955
2,000	8 r	2
1,500–2,000	50 r	3–4
1,000–1,500	350 r	28
Under 1,000	1,400 r*	128

* As such a dosage is lethal, survivors must have been protected, and the figure of estimated exposure is therefore not very reliable.

TABLE 12.

During the early nineteen fifties, reports began to come in from several sources of the development of leukaemia in both children and adults following X-ray therapy. Enough significance was attached to these reports to instigate a full scale enquiry. In 1956 this was undertaken by a committee set up by the Medical Research Council. The committee chose to investigate the incidence of leukaemia among patients who had been given X-ray treatment for a disease known as ankylosing spondylitis. As the condition affects the joints of the spine, pelvis, and shoulders treatment is extensive and amounts virtually to whole-body irradiation. A study was made of between 13,000 and 14,000 patients who had been treated between 1935 and 1954. The national death rate from leukaemia during this period was approximately 1 in 3,000: the number of cases in the group treated was some ten times greater. In order to ensure that the increased death rate from leukaemia was due directly to the X-ray therapy and not to a greater susceptibility possibly correlated with the disease, the case histories of 480 untreated patients were also investigated: no increase in the incidence of leukaemia was apparent.

ENVIRONMENTAL HAZARDS TO HEALTH 119

It may also be significant that between 1929 and 1948 the death rate from leukaemia among American radiologists was nine times greater than among other doctors. It certainly appears that ionising radiations induce leukaemia.

Another delayed effect of radiation again studied in Hiroshima and Nagasaki is the development of the severe blood disease, aplastic anaemia. Extensive radiation damage to the red bone marrow results in an inability to maintain the red blood cell count at a satisfactory level. The condition which results, aplastic anaemia, occurred less often among the bomb victims than did leukaemia: 4 cases were reported in Nagasaki in comparison with over 40 of leukaemia.

Radiation and cancer

In the young embryo the cells grow and divide regularly and repeatedly. As the body matures and the cells differentiate, the capacity for division becomes restricted and is finally lost altogether in those cells which become most highly specialised. Harmonious development demands complete integration and accurate timing of these events: at the appropriate times specific cells in certain places must cease to divide altogether and others continue to do so at a controlled rate. In some instances the power of division may be temporarily regained: this happens, for example, in response to injury and continues until the damage is repaired. The control appears to be either resident in the cell itself or exercised on it by the body as a whole: if the control is lost and division continues unchecked then the cells become malignant and the tissue is cancerous. Ionising radiations can destroy this controlling mechanism – exactly how is not fully understood – but there exists a considerable amount of evidence that such destruction does indeed take place and that exposure to radiation may be followed, usually after a very long period, by the development of cancers. The earliest recorded cases were of cancers of the skin among early radiologists who were unaware of the dangers to which they were exposing themselves. There have also been reports of cancers developing many years later among patients who received X-ray therapy in the early years before its potential danger was understood and the need for care fully appreciated.

The most conclusive evidence, however, comes from the study of the later histories of workers in certain special industries whose jobs brought them for years into contact with radioactive substances before protection was introduced. Before 1939, when standards were laid down by the International Commission on Radiological Protection, the concentration of the radioactive gas, radon, the first decay product of radium, in the atmosphere of the pitchblend ore mines in Schneeberg and Joachimsthal was thirty times greater than is now considered safe. Nearly half the men who worked in the mines during these years developed cancer of the lung, some after more than twenty years.

Radium, thorium, and the artificially produced radioactive isotopes of strontium and plutonium, if ingested, tend to be deposited in the bones, and there is a strong possibility that if they accumulate in sufficiently large quantities bone cancer may develop. The luminising industry has provided some valuable evidence. Some luminous paints contain radium and rigid controls now operate to protect those who work with it. Before this control began, however, the women who painted the dials of luminous clocks and watches were in the habit of 'pointing' their brushes in their mouths and so swallowed radium. Investigations into the later health records of these women showed that a high percentage of them sooner or later became ill and many developed cancer of the bones.

The radioactive isotope of strontium – strontium-90 – is produced in atomic explosions. Reaching the earth in fall-out it contaminates vegetation, is eaten by cows and secreted in milk. The potential danger of this was fully appreciated in 1961 when plans were ready to feed all babies on dried milk in the event of continued detonation of massive bombs by Russia.

Cancer radiotherapy

It is well known that although ionising radiations may be a direct cause of cancer, they are also used in its treatment and cure: this situation may seem somewhat paradoxical. Unlike the long-delayed cancer-producing effects of radioactivity, which are due not to destruction but to gradual modifications of the cells, radiotherapy depends upon complete cell destruction. The aim of all such treatment is the total destruction, by massive doses of radioactivity, of all malignant cells with a minimum of damage to surrounding tissues. X-rays and radium have long been used for the eradication of superficial and some deep seated cancers, and now radioactive isotopes are proving increasingly successful in the treatment of some forms of the latter. The selective absorption of iodine by the thyroid gland, for example, makes it possible to use the isotope I-131 in the treatment of cancer of the thyroid; radioactive phosphorus P-32 is prolonging the lives of sufferers from leukaemia and polyerythemia, diseases which may be regarded as cancers of the blood, the former an over-production of white cells and the latter of red.

Radiation during pregnancy

Exposure to very heavy doses of radiation results in abortion or stillbirth: in Nagasaki 23% of the pregnant women who suffered severe radiation sickness miscarried. Among those who received milder doses and who did not suffer severe radiation sickness, the rate was only 3%: high doses of radiation are apparently necessary to induce abortion. The ability of the foetus to survive moderate doses of radiation may not be altogether fortunate because irradiation which is at too low a level to produce abortion may result in the birth of a live child who is seriously defective, either mentally, physically, or both. The foetus is especially susceptible during the first three months when the organs and systems are developing: irradiation at a later date does not appear to produce deformity but results in the birth of small babies which grow into small adults. Irradiation of pregnant women for diagnostic or therapeutic purposes is a practice now avoided whenever possible: if it is essential and cannot be delayed, the doctor may consider it advisable to terminate the pregnancy.

Pesticides

Just as the radiation contaminating the atmosphere is no longer all of natural origin, but is in part man-made, so, too, the many different chemicals which now pollute the environment are not only natural substances washed out of the rocks, but also the synthetic creations of the mind of man, given reality in his laboratories. Many of these are poisons whose potential dangers are not yet fully understood.

Synthetic chemicals in the form of dusts, sprays, and aerosols are in general use in the home and garden and on the farm in the unending war against insect pests and weeds. The chlorinated hydrocarbons, DDT and Dieldrin, and the organic phosphorous compounds, malathion and parathion, are familiar as insecticides to every housewife, gardener, and farmer. Those who read the details on their bottles and packets of patent weed-killers know 'diniteo' and 'penta' too.

These substances are lethal to insects and to weeds because they enter into the very substance of the cells of these animals and plants and disrupt the fundamental metabolic processes upon which life itself depends. The possible danger lies in the fact that many of these compounds, especially the insecticides, are non-selective and may be lethal both to their intended victims and to other forms of life as well. Continued application may therefore upset the natural balance of the environment: toxic chemicals introduced at any point into the food web may result in far-reaching destruction of life. Fish and birds may be included among the ultimate victims; and the potential danger to man himself cannot be ignored. How much of the toxic material man may accumulate in his tissues, and how far such an accumulation is a potential danger, we do not know. Perhaps as with radiation, caution should be exercised.

Tobacco smoking

Some brief may, perhaps, be held for the unleashing of the dangers to health so far described, in that they have arisen as unfortunate and unforeseen by-products of man's honest attempts to increase his food supply or to add to his material comforts. The next hazard to be described – the contamination of the lungs by the hydrocarbons present in the tar from tobacco smoke – cannot make such a claim.

The possibility of a relationship between lung cancer and tobacco smoking is a subject of immense topical interest. All enquiries into the smoking habits of patients with confirmed cancer—and there have been many – show that there are many more heavy smokers among those with cancer of the lungs than among those with cancer of any other organ. Between 1951 and 1956 an important enquiry was carried out among 40,000 doctors in this country by Doll and Bradford-Hill. A brief summary of the results of this investigation is given in Table 13. The death rate from lung cancer was higher among cigarette than among pipe smokers. Death from chronic bronchitis, peptic ulcer, and pulmonary tuberculosis also showed a steady

| Group | Deaths per 1,000 | |
Tobacco smoked per day	Lung cancer	All other cancers
Non-smokers	0·07	2·04
Light smokers – up to ½ oz	0·47	2·02
Medium smokers – ½ oz to 3 oz	0·86	2·02
Heavy smokers – over 3 oz	1·66	2·02

TABLE 13.

increase from the first to the fourth group. Doll and Bradford-Hill contend that although this evidence is not proof, nevertheless it is sufficient to denote a cause-and-effect relationship.

Another important enquiry was carried out by Stocks and Campbell who published their findings in 1955. They studied the death rate from lung cancer among men between the ages of forty-five and seventy-four years living in two different areas, one rural (North Wales) and one Urban (Liverpool). Their findings are summarised in Table 14.

| | Death rate per 1,000 per year | |
	North Wales	Liverpool
Non smokers	0·14	1·13
Pipe smokers	0·41	1·43
Cigarette smokers –		
Light (less than 100 per week)	1·53	2·97
Medium (100 to 249 per week)	2·13	2·87
Heavy (over 250 per week)	3·03	3·94

TABLE 14.

These results are in agreement with those of the previous investigations and go further in suggesting that some environmental factor, which is more effective in industrial than in rural areas, is also operative. This may well be atmospheric pollution.

One of the most extensive investigations of all has been carried out by the Advisory Committee to the Surgeon General of the Public Health Service of the United States Department of Health Education and Welfare. They published their report in 1964. The report is a detailed discussion of a possible causal relationship between cigarette smoking and death, not only from lung cancer, but also from chronic bronchitis and coronary artery disease, all of which are on the increase in the United States of America – the death rate from lung cancer having increased from 18,000 in 1950 to 41,000 in 1962, heart disease from 396,000 to 578,000 in the same period of time, and chronic bronchitis from 2,300 to 15,000 between 1945 and 1962. At the same time the consumption of cigarettes has risen sharply as Table 15 shows.

Consumption per head of the population over 15 years old

1930	1,400 p.a.
1940	1,900 p.a.
1950	3,300 p.a.
1961	4,000 p.a.

TABLE 15.

68% of the male population and 32% of the female population over eighteen years of age are regular cigarette smokers.

During the American investigation, information was collected from nearly one and a quarter million men, giving significance to the findings. The subjects included both smokers and non-smokers and a number of comparisons were made. One valuable yard-stick used in the comparisons was the mortality ratio which measures the relative death rates of smokers and non-smokers: if the death rates are the same then the ratio is 1·0, if that of smokers is twice that of non-smokers then the ratio is 2·0. Table 16 summarises the results obtained.

Cause of death	Mortality ratio
All causes	1·68
Lung cancer	10·8
Bronchitis	6·1
Cancer of the larynx	5·4
Cancer of the oesophagus	3·4
Peptic ulcer	2·8
Coronary artery disease	1·7
Other heart and circulatory diseases	2·6

TABLE 16.

The death rates among the smokers increases significantly with the number of cigarettes smoked:

Number of cigarettes per day	Mortality ratio
Less than 10	1·4
11 to 19	1·7
20 to 39	1·9
40 and over	2·2

TABLE 17.

Among cigar and pipe smokers the ratio is 1·0.

One fact emerges clearly from all investigations: cigarette smokers suffer a risk of lung cancer which increases with the number of cigarettes smoked. Air pollution may be a contributory cause, but cigarette smoking is almost certainly the over-riding factor: Finland with clean air but high cigarette consumption has the next highest death rate to the British Isles and British smokers have a higher death rate per cigarette than smokers in clean air countries.

The cancer inducing, or carcinogenic substances, involved in cigarette smoking are thought to be the tars produced by condensation of the smoke. Tar from tobacco smoke contains at least seven hydrocarbons, each of which has been shown to be carcinogenic in rats: the potency of these carcinogens appears to be increased in the cigarette by the presence of other non-carcinogenic substances which would be harmless alone. Other components of cigarette smoke inhibit ciliary action in the lung which seriously interferes with the removal of foreign debris.

If cigarette smoking ceased in Great Britain, some 12,000 lives would be saved every year. It must be remembered, however, that tobacco is, to many, an effective solace: deprived of it, man might turn to other even more harmful tranquillisers.

Reference has already been made to the possible connection between cigarette smoking and coronary heart disease, a condition which is occurring with increasing frequency in Western Europe and in North America. In the United Kingdom it topped the poll in 1960 as the greatest killer of all, causing nearly 92,000 deaths. There is a certain amount of evidence that one predisposing factor is a diet high in animal fat: another may be lack of physical activity. The best preventative appears to be a low fat diet, plenty of exercise, and no smoking. For those to whom this may seem a somewhat bleak programme, the information contained in Table 18 may provide some mite of consolation.

High wine drinking countries	Annual death rate from coronary disease per 100,000 of the population
France	106
Italy	120
Switzerland	173
Germany	194
Low wine drinking countries	
U.S.A.	660
Canada	550
New Zealand	492
Finland	483
England and Wales	372

TABLE 18.

CHAPTER VI

Congenital Abnormalities

Congenital diseases are those which are already present at birth, and these may be either inherited or acquired during pre-natal life. Inherited diseases and defects already recognisable at birth include haemophilia, mongolism, and many skeletal and neural abnormalities. The agents responsible for these conditions are the genes contributed by the parents to the zygote, which, in association with their environment, control its entire development, catalysing – directly or indirectly, as they are known to do – the metabolic activities which result in tissue growth (see Vol. 1). We may assume that in these cases their mutant nature has resulted in abnormal metabolism in some region of the embryo with subsequent abnormal development.

Acquired congenital diseases may also have a known cause. A baby may be born deaf or defective in some other way because his mother was infected with the German measles virus early in her pregnancy. If a pregnant woman has syphilis, the causal organism may be transmitted via the placenta to the umbilical vessels and so to the foetus: the baby is then born with congenital syphilis – a serious and distressing disease.

Other babies may start life with some defect due to birth injury. Spastic paralysis, a condition which can be completely crippling, is often the result of injury to the brain at birth. Many other congenital deformities, from a cleft palate to gross skeletal deformity, may be present at birth for no clearly recognisable reason.

Increased knowledge will in time decrease the incidence or severity of many congenital defects. A few years ago the Rhesus baby had only a poor chance of survival: now his future is virtually assured.

Repair of lesions in children with congenital heart defects is now routine surgery in children's hospitals all over the country: children previously condemned to a life of invalidism often lead normal happy lives. A close correlation was found between the high concentrations of oxygen in the tents in which premature babies were reared and the subsequent blindness of these babies – a condition previously thought to be due to vitamin E deficiency. Blindness from this cause is now prevented.

Continued research will no doubt lead to a decrease in the incidence of, and an improved prognosis for, many other congenital diseases, and still greater help in surmounting those difficulties which beset the premature baby in the half-and-half world in which he spends the first few weeks of his life.

Abnormal growth, then, may be due to one of two major causes; defects in the genetic plan, or adverse environmental factors. It may also be due to an interaction between genetic plan and environment, neither of which alone would have affected growth adversely.

Defects in the genetic plan

Abnormalities due to defects in the genetic plan usually remain unchanged throughout life. While some, for instance, albinism (Plate 11) and polydactyly, are clearly apparent at birth, others, such as red-green colour blindness, though present at birth, are not recognised until much later, while others still, like Huntington's chorea, do not become evident until late in adult life. There are two main causes of hereditary defects: the presence of either specific mutant genes, or of chromosome abnormalities.

Defects due to the presence of mutant genes. If the zygote contains one dominant gene or a pair of recessive genes, causing a specific defect, that defect will appear in the individual formed from the zygote. Many anatomical abnormalities, such as brachy- and polydactyly, are caused by the action of dominant genes, the gene for albinism is recessive, haemophilia and red-green colour blindness are due to sex-linked recessive genes. An extremely serious condition in children caused by a dominant gene is achuloric jaundice. The red blood cells, which are abnormally shaped, are unusually fragile and destroyed too fast: as a result the child becomes anaemic, due to lack of red blood corpuscles, and jaundiced as the abundant bile pigments formed by the excess breakdown of haemoglobin accumulate in the blood.

The condition can be controlled by removal of the spleen but the genetic defect is *not* cured and can be handed on to the next generation.

Phenylketoneria, a rare and serious genetic disease, is due to the action of a recessive gene.[1] The patient is unable to utilise the amino acid, phenylalanine, formed by the digestion of dietary proteins: the phenylalanine accumulates in the blood and has a disastrous effect upon the developing brain, resulting in severe mental deficiency. Most hopeful and encouraging results have been obtained by feeding the patient on a specialised phenylalanine-free diet: if the condition is diagnosed in the first six weeks it is hoped that treatment may prove one hundred per cent successful. Diagnosis is simple: the urine contains phenylalanine, and its presence may be detected by pressing onto the wet napkin, a card treated with a suitable indicator. Out of some 10,000 babies tested annually at a Birmingham clinic two or three are found to be affected: probably some forty to fifty are born in this country every year. It must be stressed again, however, that treatment corrects the condition but does not alter its genetic cause: these treated children are, as the condition is recessive, bound to hand on one defective gene to any children which they may have.

Defects due to chromosome abnormalities. Some of the most interesting recent work in this field has been concerned with the cause of Mongolism. Mongols are defective children who show a number of clearly defined abnormalities. The head is flattened antero-posteriorly and the brain is malformed resulting in serious mental retardation. The appearance of the face is very characteristic – the slanting eyes with a pronounced skin fold and the forwardly directed nostrils are features typical of the Mongoloid peoples and give the condition its name. Other peculiarities are usually also present: the tips of the fingers may be incurved, there is often a small umbilical hernia and muscle tone is frequently poor. About 40% of Mongol children also have a malformed heart and this may lead to early death. The children are retarded in every way and do not usually progress beyond the level of a normal seven year old: sooner or later they need institutional care. It is doubtless

---

1. For details of genetic abnormalities and their mode of inheritance – see Volume I.

some consolation to their parents that Mongol children are usually tractable and affectionate and often very attractive.

A detailed study of their chromosome constitution[1] has shown that many Mongols possess an extra chromosome, 47 instead of the usual 46: the twenty-first 'pair' consists of three members. Further research has shown that the extra chromosome is contributed by the ovum: failure of the two members of the twenty-first pair of chromosomes to separate during meiosis (see Vol. I) has resulted in one cell with 24 chromosomes and one with 22, a phenomenon known as non-disjunction. If the ovum with 24 chromosomes is fertilised the resulting zygote has 47 chromosomes and develops into a Mongol baby. Non-disjunction of this type is more likely to happen during ovum formation in an ageing ovary: this explains the higher incidence of Mongolism among the children of older mothers (Plate 12).

But younger mothers do have Mongol babies and in one instance, at least, such a baby born to a twenty-two-year-old mother, had apparently the usual number of 46 chromosomes. Detailed investigation revealed, however, that the extra twenty-first chromosome was present but attached to one member of of pair number 15, a process known as translocation. The family tree of one family containing such translocation Mongols is given in Figure 9:

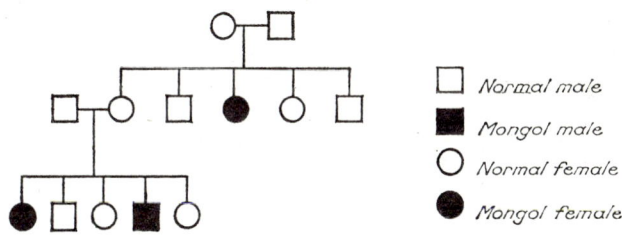

FIG. 9. A mongol family tree

Study of the chromosomes of the normal individuals showed that they had apparently only 45 chromosomes: in fact, 46 were present but translocation had occurred and one number

---

1. Chromosomes are usually studied in samples taken from the red bone marrow which contains the rapidly dividing progenitors of the blood corpuscles.

21 was attached to one number 15. In the Mongol children, however, although there were apparently only 46 chromosomes, an extra number 21 was present attached to one number 15: this was responsible for the Mongolism.

Other examples of chromosome abnormalities associated with defects of various types have been described: in one case where a malformed spine was associated with dwarfism, only 45 chromosomes were present and there was no evidence of translocation. In another instance an individual, externally female but with only one X chromosome, had no ovaries, and yet another with two X chromosomes and a Y had male accessory organs but the testes failed to develop.

Chromosome abnormalities leading to defects in development appear to be relatively common: it is estimated, for example, that the incidence of Mongolism is as high as one in every 600 babies born.

Chromosome abnormalities and leukaemia

Detailed examination of the chromosomes in the white blood cells of patients with myeloid leukaemia has shown that in some at least of the cells in the bone marrow, one chromosome of pair 21 has lost part of its substance. In some patients the new chromosome pattern appears when the disease becomes acute. The significance of this chromosome abnormality is not yet understood.

Congenitally acquired defects

Abnormalities due to environmental factors may arise before, during, or after birth: the first two types are congenital. It is often difficult to tell whether congenital conditions are inherited or acquired: this may be very important to parents, particularly if it is their first baby who is defective, as it will have a considerable influence upon their policy concerning further children. If the defect is due to some non-recurrent environmental factor operating pre-natally, then there is no need for anxiety: if on the other hand the abnormality results from the action of some recessive gene, the chances of other children being similarly affected are considerable. In some instances, a congenital condition may be due to the unfortunate interaction of certain genes and a particular environmental condition: probably the best known example is the Rhesus baby. Again, likelihood of the condition recurring is considerable: foreknowledge of this possibility may be important in saving the baby's life.

The causes of congenitally acquired abnormalities are many and various; many are unknown or little understood.

Definite proof that the foetus can be adversely affected by drugs taken by the mother came late in 1961. The drug in question was thalidomide, produced in Germany in 1955 and first marketed in this country in 1958. It was prescribed as a sedative and was reported to have no toxic properties. Some of the mothers who took the drug during early pregnancy – the 25th to the 40th days seem to be the most vital – gave birth to babies with faulty or missing limbs. According to Dr Hepp of the University of Münster orthopaedic clinic, Westphalia, the drug disturbs the metabolism of folic acid and this in turn interferes with the differentiation of the unspecialised embryonic tissue. Particularly affected are the primitive limb buds, the tissue forming the centre of the face, the outer ear, the eye, the heart, and the alimentary canal. 1,500 cases, half of whom died, have been reported in Westphalia alone: in Dr Hepp's clinic are 515 babies with short deformed arms and legs like the flippers of a seal. There are known to be at least 500 such babies in this country. Within a week of the discovery of the dangers of the drug in 1961, it was withdrawn from the market in this country and in Germany: the last babies to be affected were born in August 1962. The drug was rigorously tested before being put on the market: on rats for toxicity, on cats for adverse effects on blood pressure, on rabbits to see if it produced fever, and on guinea pigs for any allergic properties. It was not tested for its effects on the foetus; no test animal satisfactory for this purpose has yet been discovered and the harmful effects of any drug on the foetus of an animal cannot be taken to predict what would happen in the case of a woman. This discovery, that a drug, thoroughly tested and apparently perfectly safe, can harm the foetus so tragically means that none but the most essential drugs should be taken during pregnancy. Such a 'man-made catastrophe' (Dr Hepp in *Rehabilitation*) must never occur again.

If a mother contracts some infection during pregnancy, the foetus may be adversely affected. Fortunately the placenta is impermeable to bacteria: bacteria infecting the mother therefore do not reach the foetus. Not so, unfortunately, with the viruses: maternal virus infection is a potential danger to the baby. The effect of the infection on the foetus depends upon its age: the second and the first half of the third months are the most dangerous times, because this is when the organs are being laid down. The classic work in this field is that of Gregg of Australia on maternal rubella (German measles). He discovered that 86% of pregnant women who, during a major epidemic of rubella in 1941, were affected while in the second or third month of their pregnancy, gave birth to children with congenital cataract. Further investigation has shown that the infection can also cause defects in ears, heart, and brain: the organ affected is the one which was developing at the time of the infection. A woman who is exposed to German measles during early pregnancy may now be protected by an injection of gamma globulins which appear to help her to resist the disease. It is also possible that the chickenpox virus and the organism used in smallpox vaccination (see Chapter 3) can also do harm if introduced during the second month of pregnancy.

Maternal infections which occur during the first month probably result in the death of the foetus, while those which affect the mother after the third month do not result in malformation because the organs and systems are already formed.

Although the placenta normally acts as a barrier to bacteria and protozoa, it is possible for the placenta itself to become infected and damaged so that the bacterial or protozoan infection spreads to the foetus. A heavy infection will lead to the death of the foetus; a less severe one may result in the birth of a baby (see Vol. I) suffering from the particular disease. This happens very occasionally when the mother suffers from tuberculosis, but more often when she has syphilis. Congenital syphilis is, however, preventable if the mother seeks treatment early in pregnancy.

The question of the relationships between exposure to radiation and genetic abnormalities is discussed in Volume I: its effects upon the child and adult were considered more fully in Chapter V. At this point the possible consequences to the child of pre-natal exposure to radiation will be considered briefly. The assessment of the results of radiation on pre-natal development has been made chiefly by appraisal of the effects of the atom bomb explosions at Nagasaki and Hiroshima upon children born to women who were pregnant at the time, and also from the study of the children of expectant mothers who were irradiated for therapeutic or diagnostic reasons before the dangers of this practice were fully appreciated. Again, the first three months of pregnancy are the danger period: malformations of many types have been observed in the children born to women exposed to radiation during this period. Especially serious are various, often drastic, skeletal abnormalities and severe under-development of the brain with accompanying mental deficiency. The possible relationship between pre-natal exposure to radiation and the subsequent incidence of leukaemia is still under investigation.

Congenital abnormalities due to the interaction of heredity and environment

Some congenital conditions are due to interaction between a particular genetic constitution and certain pre-natal environmental factors. One of the clearest examples of this situation is the development of a Rhesus baby. The baby who suffers from an acute form of jaundice at birth, is always Rhesus positive (see Vol. I and page 103). The condition arises when a Rhesus positive baby is carried by a Rhesus negative mother and a small defect develops in the placenta. Exactly why this set of circumstances may have such disastrous consequences, how the baby is affected, and what steps are taken to alleviate the condition is discussed in Chapter IV: the point to be appreciated in this connection is that though neither of these conditions, the genetic or the environmental, would alone prove dangerous, it is the two occurring together which can have such alarming consequences. Prompt attention to the baby at birth enables the defect to be put right.

The effects of prematurity

A baby is regarded as premature if it weighs less than $5\frac{1}{2}$ lb. at birth: often, though not always, such babies are not full term. Twins and triplets are often premature, so too are malformed babies, and those born to ailing mothers, or those of poor physique, or from unsatisfactory social and economic backgrounds. Babies of 5 to $5\frac{1}{2}$ lb. are usually reared quite successfully, those weighing over $4\frac{1}{2}$ lb. have a good chance of survival.

Improved techniques have led to a considerable increase in the chance of survival of very small premature babies: many weighing as little as 2 lb. now live. In a particular Edinburgh hospital, the percentage of babies weighing 3 lb. or less who survive has increased from 4·5 in 1945 to 28·5 in 1954. The survival rate for babies of birthweight 3 to $3\frac{1}{2}$ lb. has increased from 35 to 73% during the same period.

Recent work suggests that the premature baby is at some disadvantage both immediately after birth and during childhood, with a possible legacy carried on into adult life, while for the very small baby – under 3 lb. birth weight – the disadvantages are considerable. C. M. Dillen reports in 1958 on the progress of a group of 74 babies of 3 lb. or less birth weight as follows.

7·7% died before the age of 2 years
50% had visual defects
8% were spastic

At five years old the children's intelligence was assessed as follows:

Normal or superior intelligence 37%
Dull 34%
High grade defective 18%
Grossly defective 11%

The percentage of backward and physically defective children is considerably higher than that for the population as a whole.

One very important point emerges from these investigations: as the number of very small babies who survive is steadily increasing, and as these babies are more likely to be physically or mentally handicapped than are babies of heavier birth weight, every effort must be made to reduce the incidence of prematurity. This obviously necessitates the fullest possible investigation into its causes.

Defects caused during birth

The most serious damage which the foetus can sustain during birth is damage to the brain. Some moulding of the skull normally occurs during birth: the bones of the skull are loosely attached one to another and as the baby passes down the birth canal they are pushed by pressure into an overlapping position. No damage is done to underlying tissues.

In difficult, prolonged deliveries, however, and in premature babies where the cerebral vessels are fragile, pressure may result in intracranial haemorrhages. This may result in damage to the brain and the baby may consequently be mentally defective or spastic. Regular ante-natal examination is important to determine whether or not normal delivery of the baby is possible and to be expected. The majority of abnormal deliveries can be anticipated in this way: often the abnormality can speedily be corrected or if this is not possible the baby can be delivered safely without damage by Caesarean section. Defects due to birth injury have been, and will continue to be, reduced as obstetric techniques improve.

Infection during birth

Normally the foetus grows and develops in a sterile environment, but once the membranes have been ruptured the baby is exposed to infection by any organisms which may be present in the birth canal. Severe infection may result in the death of the foetus: the most serious non-fatal situation is infection of the eyes by staphylococci or streptococci present in the vagina or by the causal agent of gonorrhoea whose normal habitat is the vagina. The resulting infection, ophthalmia neonatorum, may if untreated result in permanent blindness. Preventive treatment is, however, simple and effective: if the infant's eyes are thoroughly cleansed immediately after delivery of the head before they have even opened, the disastrous consequences of infection are avoided. This is now a routine measure after all deliveries.

But many congenital abnormalities are still unaccounted for. We do not always know, for example, why the brain fails to develop, resulting in mental deficiency, or why the units from which the face develops (see Vol. I) fail to unite and so cause hare lip or cleft palate. The faults may be inherited and in time come to be attributed to as yet unknown genes, or they may be acquired and eventually become traceable to some, at present, unsuspected pre-natal influences.

CHAPTER VII

Man and his Food

The problems of undernourishment and malnutrition
From his earliest days man has been well aware that his health and strength depend upon his having enough to eat. Food-getting – hunting, agriculture and animal husbandry – have been his main preoccupations since the beginning of history. Since the beginning of history too, there have been great changes and much variety in man's feeding habits: there have always been periods of plenty and times of scarcity; there have always been those who live well and those who fare badly. Never has this been more true than it is today: we in this country have become increasingly aware during recent years that, while a large proportion of the world's population enjoys a diet which is at least adequate and often abundant, there are many millions more who go hungry, who suffer from undernourishment or malnutrition or both. Some estimates put this figure as high as 1,500 million people – half the total population of the world. Not only the sadness but also the significance of this is tremendous. In the words of the Food and Agriculture Organisation of the United Nations' publication *Six Billion to Feed* –

> The magnitude of the problem and the continuing inadequacy of food production in the 'hungry regions' of the world present a challenge to all who think in terms of a better and a peaceful world. Such a world is impossible in the present circumstances. A hungry man is a social liability. He cannot work effectively on an empty stomach; he cannot study and learn as he must to improve his condition of life; he cannot think beyond his immediate needs, of which food is dominant; he cannot build up resistance to disease; and in short, because he can be counted in millions, he retards not only the economic and social development of his country, but also the prosperity of the world.

It is obvious that here is a problem of global proportions which can be tackled only by worldwide efforts. If such methods are to be effective they must be based on a thorough scientific investigation into the detailed nature of the problem: where the hungry people live, how many of them there are, whether they are underfed or malnourished or both, what food is available to them, how much more they need and how it can best be produced. Such an investigation has recently been carried out by the F.A.O. as part of their Freedom from Hunger campaign.

A good diet is one which is both quantitatively and qualitatively adequate: it meets the body's calorie needs, it contains enough and sufficiently varied proteins, and it is sufficiently rich in all mineral and vitamin requirements. Those whose diet is quantitatively inadequate do not get enough to eat and live on a diet which is deficient in calories: they suffer from undernourishment and are actually hungry. Probably between 300

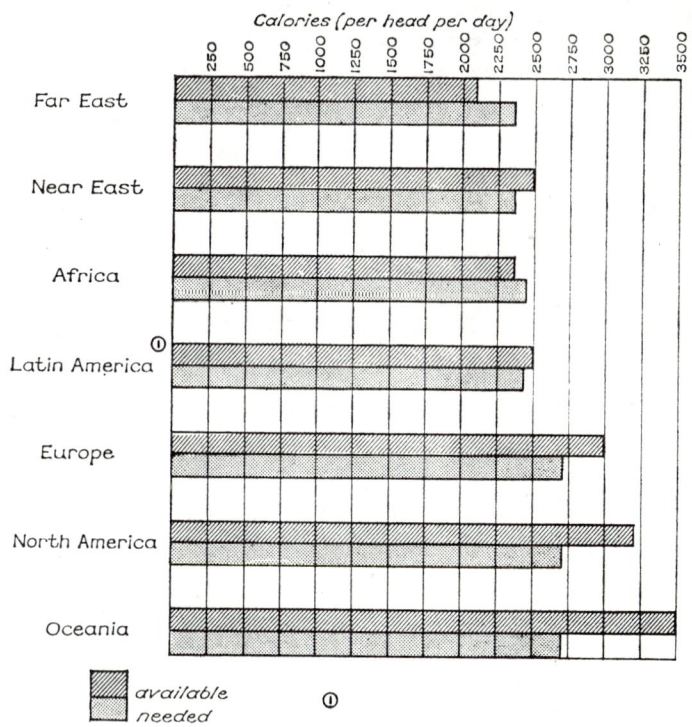

FIG. 10. Calorie levels in different regions.

and 500 million people in the world today are underfed. Those who live on a diet with too high a proportion of starchy foods and too few protective foods – proteins and vitamins – suffer from malnutrition. Undernourishment and malnutrition often go hand in hand: the food which the undernourished do get – potatoes and cereals – contains too much starch and too little meat, milk, fruit, and vegetables – the protective foods.

Calories needed and available

In order to assess the extent of world undernourishment, the F.A.O. made an extensive enquiry into the calorie requirements and the calorie intake of large numbers of people in many different parts of the world. Calorie requirements in excess of intake for any length of time denote hunger. Intake is obviously related directly to the quantity of food eaten: requirements depend upon sex, age, weight, climate, environment, and physical activity and therefore vary considerably from individual to individual and from country to country. The findings of the F.A.O. enquiry are shown in Figure 10.

Study of Table 19 shows that the countries can be divided into two groups.

	Countries	*Calories available (average)*	*Calories needed (average)*
GROUP I			
The low calorie countries	The Far East The Near East Africa Latin America*	2,175	2,375
GROUP II			
The high calorie countries	Europe North America Oceania	3,050	2,650

* Argentine, Uruguay, and Paraguay come into Group II.

TABLE 19.

In Figure 11 the size of the countries in the two groups is shown in relation to their population: the inference is obvious. 2,136 millions live in the countries of Group I, 876 millions in those of Group II. There is of course considerable individual variation among the people of the countries in the two groups: some people in Group I countries have an intake above their

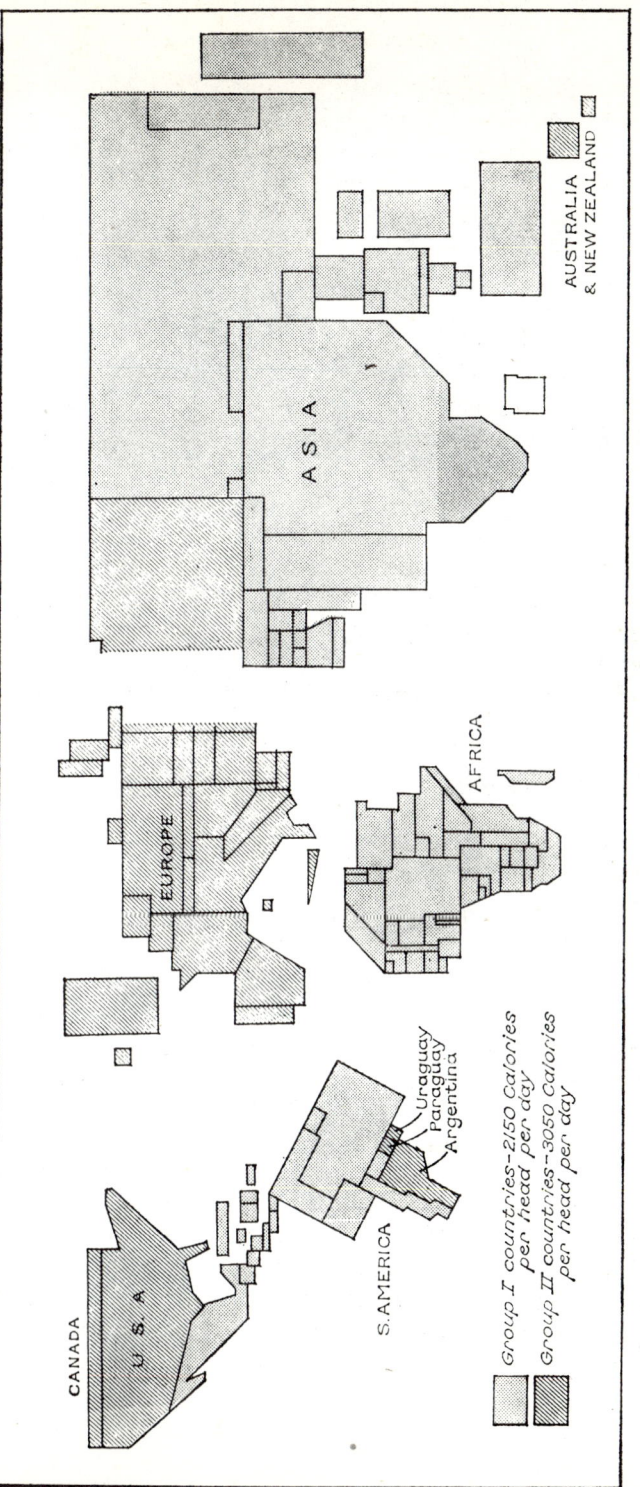

FIG. 11. World calorie supplies. (Size of countries shown in relation to 1960 population.)

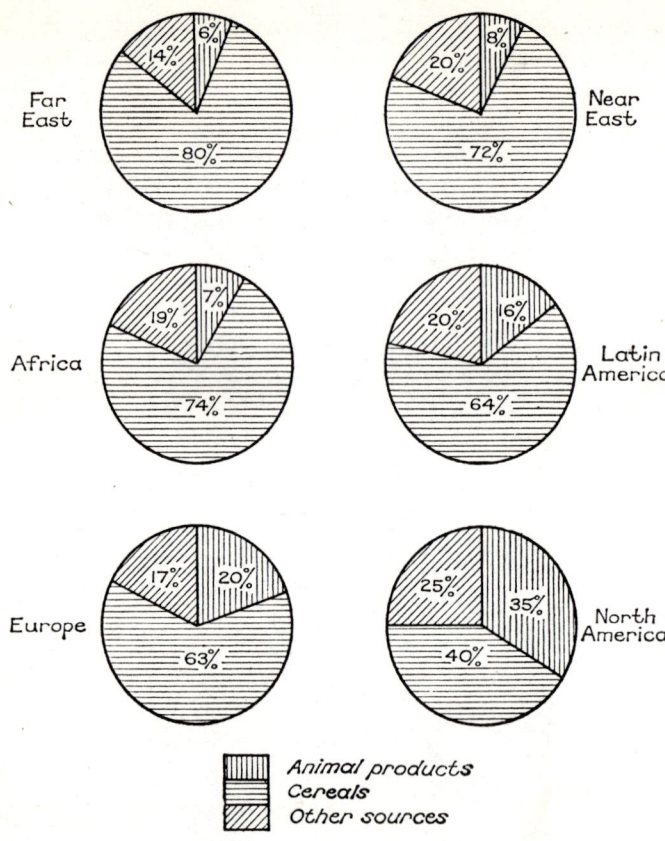

FIG. 12. Source of calories.

needs, while some in Group II do not receive enough. The final assessment is that, in the early 1960's, between 300 and 500 million people in the world were hungry.

Persistent undernourishment is very debilitating and is inevitably associated with a high degree of infection. An inadequate supply of calories leads to loss of weight, lethargy, and decreased work output. The latter is serious not only for the individual concerned but also for the economy of the community.

In Figure 12, a more detailed analysis is given of the types of food from which the calories are obtained in six regions for which data is available. It will be seen that in the regions belonging to Group I a very high percentage of the calories come from cereals, starchy roots, and sugar, and a very low proportion from animal products. The significance of this is discussed later in the chapter.

If the composition of the diet of the two groups is further analysed, the same point is once again clear: the diet of the Group I countries is not only too low in calories but also in fats and in proteins, especially those of animal origin (Figs. 13, 14, 15).

These two characteristics of a diet – the proportion of calories obtained from cereals, starchy roots, and sugar, and the quantity of animal protein which it contains – are useful indicators of its quality. Any diet in which the proportion of calories derived from cereals, starchy foods, and sugar is high and the intake of animal protein is low may be considered to be unbalanced: those who live on such a diet for any length of time suffer from malnutrition.

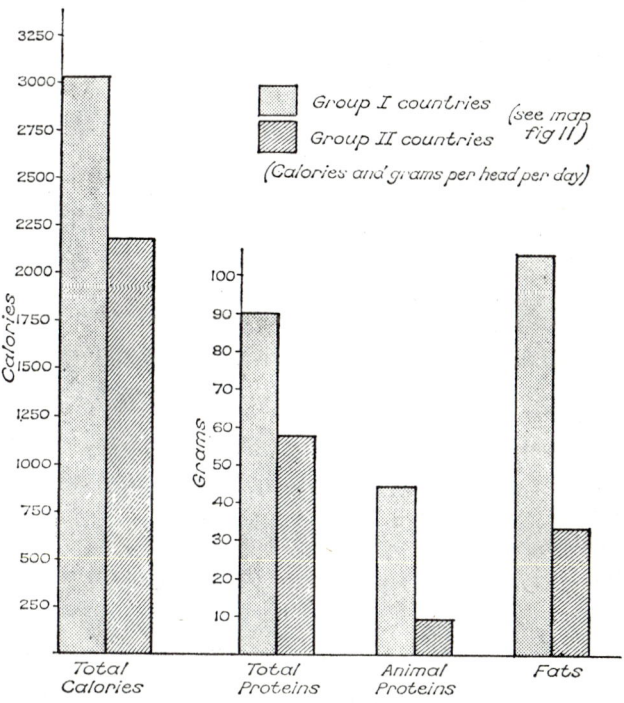

FIG. 13. Food consumption by Group I and Group II countries.

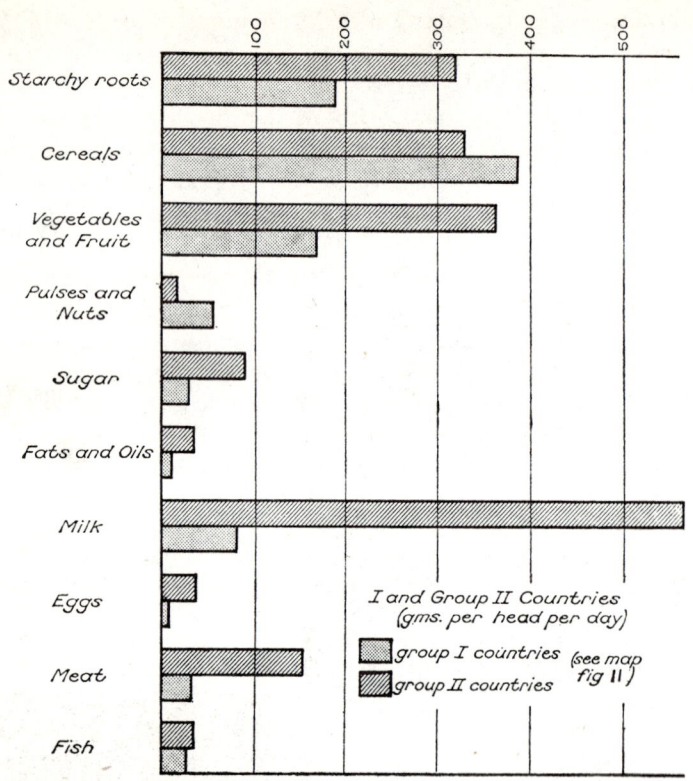

FIG. 14. Analysis of food consumption by Group I and Group II countries.

Protein deficient diets are generally also short of vitamins and minerals; such deficiencies lead to the incidence of deficiency diseases. As may be expected, these are far more widespread in the countries of Group I than in those of Group II.

The most widespread and one of the most serious of the deficiency diseases is kwashiorkor caused by protein deficiency. This disease which affects young children when they are weaned on to an unbalanced diet, results in wasting, oedaema, degeneration of the liver, and sores on the skin: protein deficiency is also associated with increased susceptibility to tuberculosis and dysentery. Specific deficiency diseases associated with lack of particular vitamins, include beri-beri, pellagra, scurvy, xerophthalmia blindness, and rickets. These diseases,

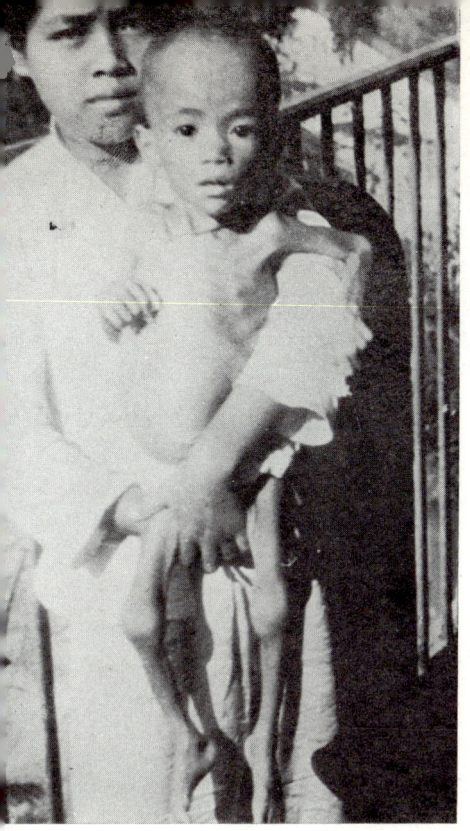

PLATE 13: Malnutrition
A Vietnamese victim

(*a*) Before treatment

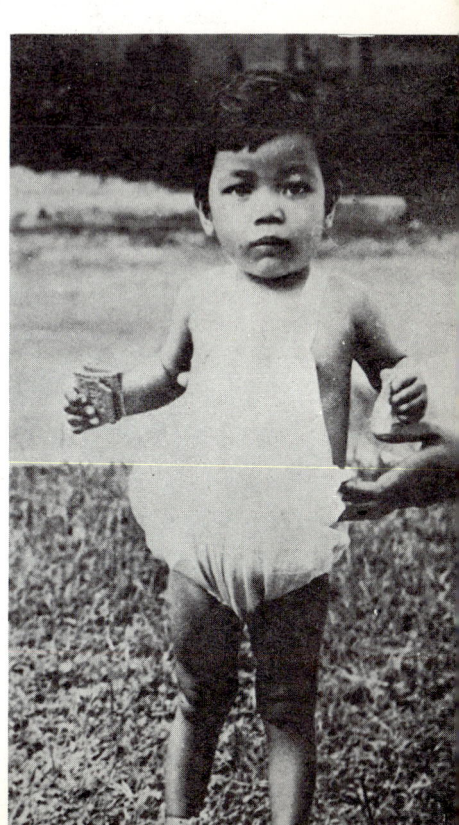

(*b*) After treatment

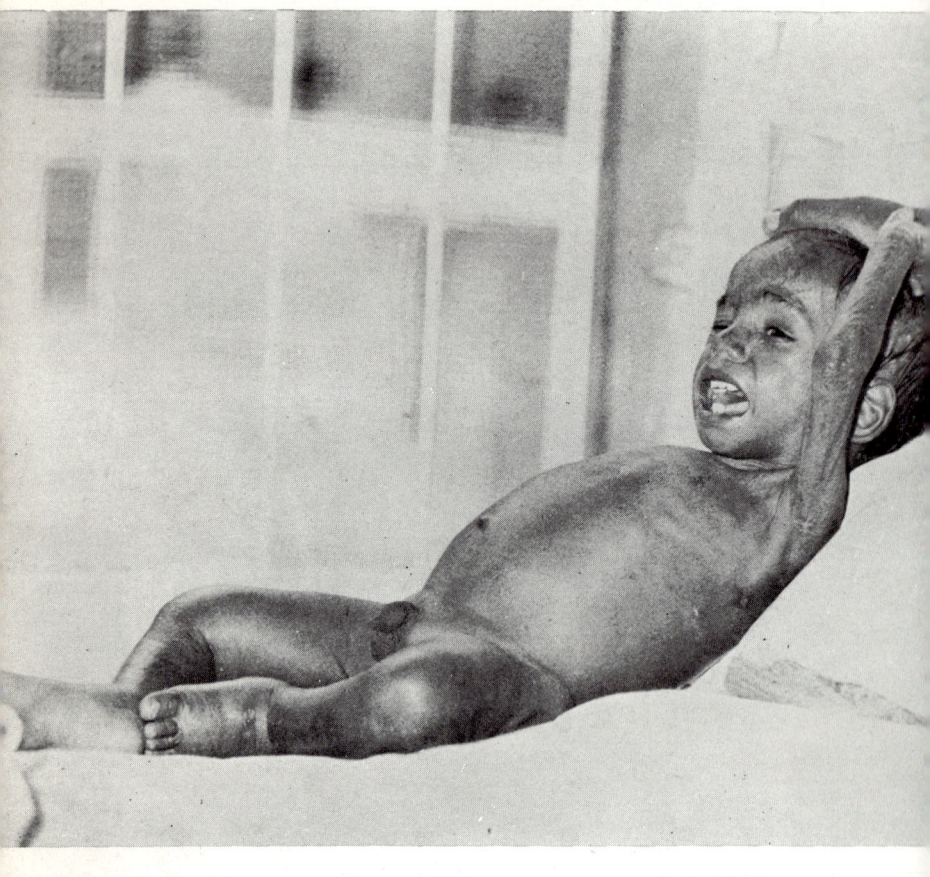

PLATE 14: A severe case of Kwashiorkor—18-month-old Govidaswany from Madras state. Govidaswany was found in time and nursed back to health

PLATE 15: Man against the desert. The Nubian desert on the banks of the Nile. Even in country composed entirely of rocks and sand man has cultivated a tiny tract of land

PLATE 16: Conquering the desert

(a) The parched, cracked earth of the Turkmenjstan desert in Soviet Central Asia

(b) The second crop of cotton gathered on the land now irrigated by the Kara Kum canal

many of which are of considerable historical importance, are still common in the underdeveloped countries.

As a result of their investigations, the F.A.O. estimate that, in the early 1960's, at least one third and possibly even one half of the world's population – 1,500 million people – suffered from some form of malnutrition.

It is evident that, unless active measures are adopted, the people living in large areas of the world, particularly those of the under-developed countries, are condemned to a permanent, serious state of under-nourishment and malnutrition. If this is to be avoided then food has to be increased in quantity and in quality, the greatest need being for more fruit, vegetables, and foods of animal origin. The immediate aim is to raise the national calorie intake to eliminate the gap between

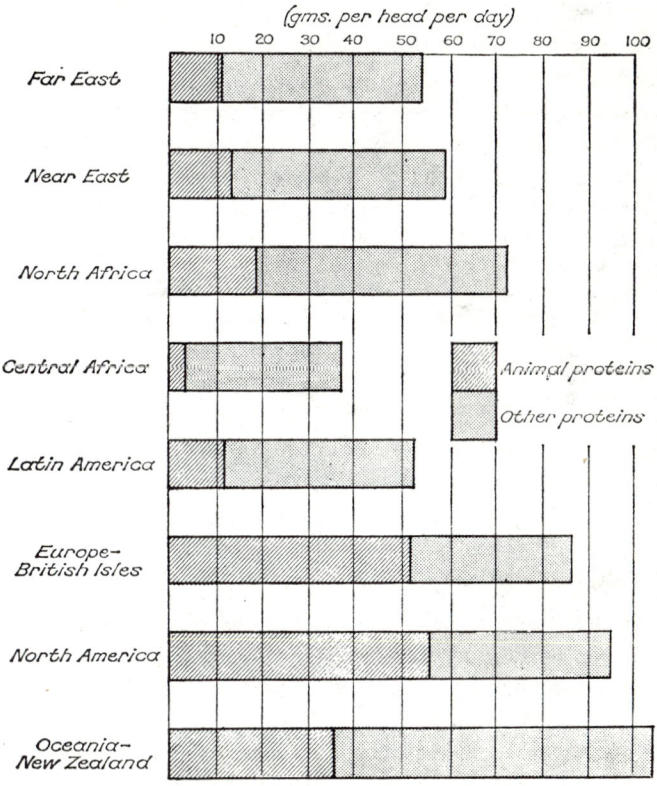

FIG. 15. Protein intake by selected countries.

national intake and national requirements; later, attempts will be made to raise the intake still further to allow for unequal distribution among the population. In this way undernutrition would be brought to an end. At the same time everything possible must be done to improve the quality of the diet and so to end malnutrition: this would be achieved if the quality of the diet was as good in all countries as it now is in those which we call developed. It is very important to appreciate that improvement in quantity must be accompanied by improvement in quality: increase in quantity alone will only serve to accentuate the existing imbalance and while temporarily alleviating hunger will lead to even greater malnutrition.

If success is to be achieved it is essential to be sure that the people concerned are able to pay the increased food bill. This may not always be so as hunger and poverty so often go hand in hand. It is also important that the changes made in the diet are not too extensive or made too rapidly: most people have conservative feeding habits and resent sudden change. Furthermore, it is not always advisable merely to increase the existing level of supplies of certain commodities in certain regions – this may only lead to further imbalance.

The immediate needs of the various Group I countries, as estimated by the F.A.O., are set out in Table 20.

	Calories per day			Proteins – grams per day		
	Present	Target	Increase	Present	Target	Increase
Far East	2,050	2,300–2,400	250–350	8	10–20	2–12
Africa	2,300	2,400–2,450	100–150	11	15–20	4–9
Near East and Latin America	2,400	2,400–2,500	—	14	20	6
Average Group I	2,150	2,500	350	9	20	11
Group II	3,060	—	—	44	—	—

TABLE 20. Immediate needs of Group I countries

The increase needed in total food production

Here we come to a point of absolutely vital importance. All the above figures are based on the present world population. But the population projections made by the United Nations forecast that the present world population of 3,000 millions will have increased to at least 6,000 millions and possibly considerably more by A.D. 2000, and that the rate of increase will be greatest in the underdeveloped countries of Group I (see

Chapter VIII). Even to maintain present levels of feeding, if the population continues to grow at the expected rate, an overall world increase in food supplies of some 120% will be necessary, with figures as high as 150% in underdeveloped countries. To bring about even the minimum improvements in these countries, as indicated in Table 20, the target will be far higher. The increase needed to achieve the medium target by A.D 1980 and the high target by A.D. 2000 are set out in Table 21.

	1980	2000
Far East	120	300
Near East	90	200
Africa	75	160
Latin America	90	240

TABLE 21. Percentage increase in total food supplies needed to achieve low target by A.D. 1980 and high target by A.D. 2000

The percentage increase needed in specific foodstuffs is estimated to be as follows

	1980	2000
Cereals	45	110
Pulses	95	200
Animal products	85	190

TABLE 22. Percentage increase in specific foodstuffs needed to achieve targets

The broad conclusion to be drawn is that, should the population grow according to the United Nations forecast, the world's total food supplies would have to be doubled by 1980 and trebled by the turn of the century in order to provide a level of nutrition reasonably adequate to the needs of all the world's peoples.

(*Six Billion to Feed*, published by F.A.O.)

CHAPTER VIII

The Population Problem

The nature of the problem

The science of demography may be considered to have been born in the year 1798 when Thomas Robert Malthus, a clergyman by profession but an economist by persuasion, published his now famous *Essay on Population*. The Malthusian doctrine which he postulated was based on two fundamental observations: that while the population increases by geometrical progression, food supplies do not; populations are therefore in danger of outgrowing their food supply. Although the natural curbs to population growth described by Malthus – 'vice and misery' – no longer operate and although the remedy which he suggested – 'moral restraint' – is no longer acceptable, yet the basic problem is unchanged: as a result of this unequal rate of increase, half the population of the world today suffer from undernourishment or malnutrition, and still the population continues to increase at an alarming rate.

Population pressures are not a new phenomenon: what is new is the scale of the present pressure in many areas of the world and the ever increasing restrictions on the way in which this pressure can be released. In the past the safety valves have been ready at hand: when a population was outgrowing its territory it could solve its problem by better use of the existing facilities, by territorial expansion, or by emigration. And always the three great natural restrictive forces – disease, famine and war – were at work. Today no such simple solution exists. Better use of existing land and the exploitation of new, often demands skill and capital which is not always readily available. Neither do natural curbs now operate so effectively. Improved maternal and child welfare services have resulted in a dramatic fall in the infant mortality rate. Infections and other diseases have been brought under control, leading to a decrease in the death rate and an increased expectation of life (Table 23).

	1950	1975 (estimated)
Total	25	17
Africa	33	29
North America	9	9
Latin America	19	12
Asia	33	19
Europe	9	10
Oceania	12	10
U.S.S.R.	7	7

TABLE 23. Death rates per 1,000

The total population of the world at the time of Christ has been estimated at about 250 to 300 millions. Today a conservative estimate is 3,000 million, an overall tenfold increase. Details of the estimated past and predicted future population and annual rate of increase for the years 1650 to 2000, are given in Tables 24 and 25.

Year, A.D.	Population in millions
1650	500–550
1750	700
1900	1,550
1925	1,907
1930	2,000
1950	2,497
1960	3,000
1975	3,828 (1957 estimate)
2000	6,267 (1957 estimate)
2000	7,410 (1963 estimate)

TABLE. 24. *Estimated and predicted world population A.D. 1650–2000*

Years	Percent increase
1650–1750	0·2
1900–1950	0·9
1958	1·7
1962	2·1
1975–2000	2·6 (1957 estimate)
	3·8 (1963 estimate)

TABLE 25. Average annual percentage increase in world population, A.D. 1650–2000

It will be seen that in the above tables two estimates are given for the year A.D. 2000: the 1957 estimate made by the United Nations is now considered to have been too conservative, and a revised estimate made in 1963 gives a considerably higher figure.

Reference to Table 26 shows that the rate of population growth is not uniform throughout the world but is greater in the underdeveloped countries of Group I where the introduction of medical services is comparatively recent. In the developed countries, the effective factors have already been in operation for some years, consequently the results have been more gradually absorbed and are less obvious.

	1900	1925	1950	1975	2000 (1957 estimate)	2000 (1963 estimate)
Total	1,550	1,907	2,497	3,828	6,267	7,410
Africa	120	147	199	303	517	860
N. America	81	126	168	240	312	388
Latin America	63	99	163	303	592	756
Asia	857	1,020	1,380	2,210	3,870	4,400
Europe	423	505	574	751	947	973
Oceania	6	10	13	21	29	33

TABLE 26. Growth of the world's population by countries between 1900 and 2000 (figures in millions)

The differences between the patterns of growth in the different countries are demonstrated even more dramatically if the average annual percentage increases for each of the twenty-five-year periods between A.D. 1900 and 2000 are considered. These are set out in Table 27.

	1900–25	1926–50	1951–75	1976–2000 (1957 estimate)	1976–2000 (1963 estimate)
Total	0.9	1.2	2.2	2.6	3.8
Africa	0.2	0.3	0.6	2.8	7.3
N. America	2.2	1.3	1.8	1.2	2.4
Latin America	2.0	2.6	3.4	3.8	5.9
Asia	0.8	1.4	2.4	3.0	3.9
Europe	0.8	0.5	1.2	1.0	1.1
Oceania	2.7	1.2	2.5	3.1	2.5

TABLE 27. Average annual percentage increase in population

The overall percentage increase for 1962 was 2·1: it was 3·5 in the countries of Group I, and 1·3 in those of Group II.

A detailed study of these figures shows that while (on the 1957 estimate, though less obviously on the 1963) in the Group II countries the rate of increase is past its maximum, those of Group I still show a steady increase in rate. On the 1963 estimate, many of the Group I countries will treble or even quadruple their population between A.D. 1900 and 2000, while those in Group II will little more than double theirs.

The most rapid rate of growth is therefore just where the problem of overpopulation and undernourishment is already most acute.

The possible solutions to the problem

If the fear of hunger is to cease to be the spectre haunting many millions of people as it is today, then the ever widening gap between world population and world food production must be narrowed and finally closed. There are basically two ways in which this can be done – world food production can be increased and distribution improved, and the growth of the population can be controlled.

Increasing world food production. A significant increase in world food production can be achieved only by full development of all resources: not only must there be an increase in total production but also a fairer distribution of available food. The latter problem is largely political and economic: the man-made barriers of world politics and economics too often make it impossible or inconvenient to share all available food supplies evenly. In America the cultivated acreage has been reduced and crops destroyed to avoid upset to her own internal economy. Such a situation and the consequent unequal distribution of resources should not be tolerated in a world where millions are underfed.

Total world production of food can be increased in two ways: land already under cultivation can be made to yield more abundantly, and new areas can be opened up for food production. In this context the possibilities of the sea and its virtually untapped potential resources should not be overlooked. Scientific agriculture and farming have done much to increase the yield per acre of land under cultivation and could do still more. The best possible farming, using all the knowledge and available resources of modern science, could possibly double the yield from land already under cultivation. The judicious use of manures and fertilisers, the creation by hybridisation of strains of plants with higher seed yield and greater resistance to disease, the control of these diseases and of animal pests, improved selective breeding and husbandry of cattle, pigs, sheep, and poultry are practices already making an ever increasing contribution to fertility wherever they are applied. The great need now is for education: those who farm the land need the opportunity to learn to do so wisely and well.

The land area of the world is some 35,700 million acres. Of this about 11,000 million acres are suitable for crops but only 3,000 to 4,000 million acres are actually under cultivation. Many of the other 7,000 to 8,000 million acres are so inaccessible that enormous capital expenditure would be necessary to open them up. In some parts of the world marginal areas have been successfully brought into production: in the U.S.S.R. and in Canada this has been made possible by the introduction of new varieties of early ripening grain which have made it feasible to grow wheat further north than ever before. In the U.S.S.R. and in Pakistan enormous irrigation schemes have brought much semi-arid land under cultivation. Many tropical areas could yield valuable products if labour, capital, and equipment were available, and suitable crops and stock could be developed (Plates 15 and 16).

Much more food could be harvested from the sea by the development of fisheries and improvement of techniques and by the cultivation of fish in suitable localities like the paddy fields of the East. Chemical food synthesis, too, might play its part – an artificial system imitating the natural photosynthetic activity of the green plant.

One of the most important factors in maintaining and increasing food production is the careful conservation of land already under cultivation. Where land is covered by natural vegetation, the natural cycle of birth, growth, and death maintain the fertility of the soil: the decaying plants and animals return the substances which they borrowed from it during their life time. Continued cropping without putting back anything soon exhausts the soil and the greatest enemy of all – soil erosion – moves in and reduces fertile soil to bare rock. The greatest barrier to erosion is vegetation: the plant roots bind the soil particles together, the plant cover checks the force of the rain and breaks that of the wind, the dead remains – humus – make the soil porous and help it to hold reserves of water. Over grazing, overcropping, and deforestation all cause accelerated erosion and loss of fertility. Man-made deserts, the result of erosion following man's misuse of the land, are scattered all over the world: some are of recent date, others are as old as history itself. The deserts of Palestine came into being in the long years of neglect which followed the fall of the Roman Empire: in New Zealand the destruction of the native bush and the introduction of non-indigenous grazing animals, has, during the last century, brought the effects of erosion to nearly one quarter of the country. These examples could be duplicated over and over again in all parts of the world: since the dawn of civilisation and throughout the ages, man's progress has been marked by the creation of desert after desert, as he continues to misuse the land which feeds him.

Control of population growth

Control of the birth rate is the basic factor in ensuring that people do not outrun resources. The problem is no longer either local or national but worldwide, yet remains essentially a highly individual and personal one.

There is nothing new in the idea of trying to prevent conception. Since Greek and Roman times men and women have tried by many different methods, some mystical, some rational, to control fertility. From time to time tokens such as amulets, golden rings, and wreaths of myrtle have been worn and strange, illogical practices have been carried out. Women have been encouraged to spit three times into the mouth of a frog, to eat dead bees, and to hold a pebble of jasper in their hands if they wished to avoid childbearing. Many other equally illogical practices are recorded in the contemporary literature of various ages.

From earliest times rational attempts to prevent conception have also been carried out. These have been aimed at influencing some known or suspected phase in or component part of the reproductive processes: basically this may be achieved at one of three points – ovulation, fertilisation, or implantation. Three thousand years ago the Egyptians were using suppositories made of camel dung to prevent fertilisation and many other ancient recipes still exist: rock salt dipped in oil and mustard seed, chopped cabbage leaves, oil and tar; honey with sodium carbonate, and honey with acacia tips are a representative sample. In the light of modern knowledge we now know that the majority of these recipes combine a spermicide with a deterrent to sperm mobility which is still the basis of the modern contraceptive pessaries.

Man has also long believed that some potion taken orally could interfere with the reproductive process. Recipes are many and various and come from all places and all ages. Some, like walnut leaves, saffron, and the foam from a camel's mouth may have been unpleasant but were fortunately harmless, others like arsenic, pills of oil of mercury, and lead-containing water were highly dangerous: none was effective in achieving the purpose for which it was intended.

In the development of contraceptives the aim has always been to find some effective method of preventing pregnancy which would make it unnecessary to take any precautions at the time of intercourse. Research in this field has resulted in two different methods: the oral contraceptive – 'the pill' – and the intra-uterine contraceptive device, – the 'I.U.C.D.' – the former prevents ovulation and the latter prevents pregnancy at some point before or at the time of implantation.

The idea of preventing ovulation as distinct from fertilisation was first suggested as long ago as 1856. However it was not until 1935 that Gregory Pincus, a research biologist from Massachusetts, discovered that a group of chemical steroids of the progestogen type, when taken orally, had the same inhibiting effect on ovulation as the natural hormones produced in the body. Over two hundred different compounds were tested on rats and rabbits until eventually it was found that the most effective substances were 19-norsteroids, derivatives of 19-nortestosterone, and that one, norethynodrel, closely related to oestrogen, was the most effective of all. These compounds were then subjected to extensive laboratory research and to extensive field tests among women of Puerto Rico and Haiti.

The compound is administered in the form of a pill: one pill is taken daily for twenty days beginning on the fifth day of the menstrual cycle: the dose is then discontinued to allow menstruation to occur – this usually takes place within one to four days. Five days later the daily pill is resumed. The exact effect of the pills is a little uncertain: they appear to act on the pituitary gland preventing the release of gonadotrophins, on the ovary, preventing maturation of the follicles in the same way as the natural hormones do during pregnancy, and on the uterus where they inhibit adequate preparation for implantation. Early pills had some side effects – nausea, dizziness, and headache but these have been largely eliminated.

During the trial period the research workers had three main anxieties: whether the compounds would remain effective after prolonged administration, whether they could possibly be carcinogenic, and whether they would decrease the possibility of conception when a baby was wanted. The tests in Puerto Rico indicate that after nine years of treatment these fears are groundless: whether or not any of them will be justified in the long run, it is too early to tell.

In 1960 a number of clinical tests were instigated in this country and in 1961 the Family Planning Association added the nine preparations which had been found to be satisfactory to their list of approved contraceptives. Except when prescribed by a doctor on medical grounds the pills, like other contraceptives cannot be obtained under the National Health Service: a month's supply costs approximately ten shillings. About 300,000 women were using this method of birth control by the end of 1964.

The intra-uterine contraceptive device is an implement introduced into and retained in the uterus to prevent pregnancy. Its contraceptive nature is not fully understood but it appears to prevent effective implantation; its presence does not dislodge a fully implanted foetus. Various types of devices have been tried out and either accepted or discarded: five are now considered satisfactory. One, the Hall-Stone ring, is of stainless steel, the others of plastic or nylon. The Lippes loop is a double S-loop of plastic, the Margulies spiral is of the same material. The Birnberg bow is an hour-glass shaped plastic device, and the Zipper ring is of nylon. The devices can be straightened for insertion through the cervix – a very great advantage – and once in the uterus they regain their shape. Once fixed the devices can be left in place, in the case of the plastic ones for years, and removed when pregnancy is wanted. Some women cannot tolerate the devices, others cannot retain them. If auxiliary medical personnel could be trained to insert the devices safely and securely this method of birth control, requiring little effort on the part of the wearer, might prove the most satisfactory of all in the underdeveloped countries: in Korea it is already planned to put one million such devices into use in the next few years.

The Medical Committee of the International Planned Parenthood Federation consider that this is a form of birth control which could be brought very quickly into widespread use and could make a major contribution to the whole problem of birth control.

Many difficulties stand in the way of a world wide programme of birth control. Many refuse to accept the use of contraceptives on religious grounds; to others the whole idea is aesthetically repugnant. But perhaps the greatest obstacle of all is ignorance: the effective use of any type of contraceptive, with the possible exception of the I.U.C.D., requires the intelligent co-operation of the people concerned and it is just where the need is greatest that ignorance, misunderstanding, and genuine inability to co-operate make the task most difficult.

And what of the population problems of this country? Perhaps there is no better way in which to conclude than in the words of Sir Joseph Hutchinson taken from his presidential address to the British Association at Nottingham on August 31st, 1966:

For, make no mistake, this country already carries a population as great as the environment can support without degeneration, and it will call for all the knowledge and skill we can command to prevent irreparable damage before we achieve a stable population, even if we set about stabilisation without delay.

This is the great remaining challenge of our time. We have mastered the physical world and the world of biology. We ourselves remain untamed. Our greatest need is to master the threat of our own numbers.

Index

Abscess, 82
Aedes aegypti, 18
   minimus, 35
Agglutination, 96
Allergy, 100
Ancylostoma duodenale, 68
Ankylosing spondylitis, X-ray treatment effects, 118
Anthrax, 42
Antibiotics, 6, 27, 91
   mode of action, 92
Antibodies, 85, 95
   theories of formation, 96–7
Antigen-antibody reactions, 95
   allergy, 100
   sensitisation, 99
Antitoxins, 85, 86
Aplastic anaemia, from radiation, 119
Asbestosis, 113
Asthma, 101
Aureomycin, 92

BCG vaccine, 90
Babies, premature, 133
Bacteria, pathogenic, 38, 39
   attack by, 41
   dates of identification, 32
   occurrence, 39–40
Bacterial infections, 38, 42
Bacteriophage T2, 52, 54
Becket, Thomas à, 7
'Benzene hexachloride' (hexachlorocyclohexane), 22
Bilharziasis, 72
Birth, defects caused during, 134
   infections during, 135
Black Death, 3
Blood flukes, 72
Blood-grouping antigens, 102
   ABO, 104

   rhesus, 103
Bronchitis, 109
Byssinosis, 115

Calories, requirements, 138–9
   sources, 140
Cancer, lung, 109, 122–3
   and radiations, 119
   radiotherapy, 120
   thyroid, radioiodine in, 121
   viruses and, 61
Carriers of diseases, 78
Cestoda, 71
Chickenpox, 57, 59
Chloromycetin, 92
Chloroquin, 22, 80
Cholera (*see also* Vibrio cholerae), 12
   outbreaks, 13–17
Chromosome abnormalities, 128
Clostridia, 43
Clostridium botulinum, 43
   tetani, 43
   welchii, 44
Coal mining, pneumoconiosis in, 113
   silicosis in, 112
Cold, common, 59
Contraceptives, 151–2
Cornea grafting, 107
Corynebacterium diphtheriae, 43
Cotton dust, 115
Cowpox, 10

DDT (pp'-dichlorodiphenyltrichloroethane), 6, 8, 22, 24
   resistance to, 23
   toxic effects, 122
Deficiency diseases, 142
Dieldrin, 22
   toxic effects, 122

INDEX

Diniteo, 122
Diphtheria, 42
  control of, 87
  immunisation, 43
Diseases, ancient Egyptian, 2
  history of, 1
Dust, 109
Dysentery, amoebic, 63
  bacilliary, 45

ELECTRON MICROSCOPE, 51
Entamoeba histolytica, 64
Epidemics, 28
Erythromycin, 92

FASCIOLEPSIS BUSKII, 71
Flukes, parasitic, 71
Food-borne diseases, 78
Food production, increasing, 149
Foot and mouth virus, 51
Foundry silicosis, 112

GANGRENE, gas, 44
Gastro-enteritis, 58
Genes, mutant, 127
Geneva Office, 32
German measles, 59
  in mothers, 132
  virus, 86
Gonococcus, 46
Granite, silicosis from, 111

HAEMOLYTIC DISEASE, 103
Haemophillus pertussis, 45
Hay fever, 101
Health, definition, 1
  in history, 1
Hepatitis, infective, 58
Herpes, 60
Herpes simplex virus, 51
Hook worm, 68
Hyaluronidase, 41

IMMUNITY, artificial, 80
Infection, clinical, pattern of, 84
Inflammation, 81-2
Influenza, 27
  epidemics, 28-9
  virus, cultivation, 54

  virus, types, 30
  variability, 59
Inoculation, 86-7
Insect-borne infections, 79
Interferon, 97

JAUNDICE, 58
  achuloric, 127
Jenner, Edward, 10, 12

KIDNEY GRAFTING, 107
Kwashiorkor, 142

LEPROSY, 47
  'law of', 2
Leukaemia, chromosome abnormalities, 130
  mouse, 61
  radiation, 118
Lymphocytes, non-phagocytic, 83

MALARIA, 21
  course of, 65
  distribution of, 21, 23
  drugs for, 80
  parasites of, 64
  Thailand programme, 34
  types and distribution, 66-7
Malathion, 122
Malnutrition, 138
Malthus, Thomas Robert, 146
Mantoux test, 90
Mass radiography, 90
Mastigophora, 63
Measles, 59
Meningitis, 44
Methisazone, 12
Mompessa, Rev. William, 4
Mongolism, 128
Montague, Lady Mary Wortley, 10
Moses, 2
Mucoproteins, 106
Mumps virus, 55, 60
Myobacterium leprae, 47
  tuberculosis, 46

NEMATHELMINTHES, 68
Nematodes, parasitic, 68, 70
Nucleic acids, in viruses, 52

INDEX

Ophthalmia neonatorum, 135
Otitis media, 44

Paludrine, 22, 80
PAM, 94
Panama Canal, yellow fever at, 18
Pandemics, 28
Parathion, 122
Paratyphoid, 45
Paris Green, 22
Paris Office, 32
Pasteur, Louis, 31
Pathogens, 38
Penicillin, 91, 94
  resistance to, 93
  in treponematoses, 94
Pesticides, hazards with, 121
Phagocytosis, 81
Phenylketonuria, 128
Philistines, plague among, 3
Pinta, 122
Plague, bubonic, 3, 46
  in Britain, 3–4
  in Europe, 5
  in London, 4
  pneumonic, 5
Plasmodia, 64–6
  pathogenic, 66
Platyhelminthes, 68, 71
Pneumoconioses, 110
  effects, 114
  in mining, 113
Poliomyelitis, 57
  course of, 57–8
  virus, 51–2, 55
Polyoma virus, 61
Population, growth, 146–8
  control, 151
Potteries, silicosis in, 111
Pregnancy, irradiation effects, 121
Prophylaxis, 80
Protozoa, pathogenic, 38, 63, 64
Puerperal fever, 44
Pus, 82

Quarantine, 31
Quinine, 22, 80

Rabies, 76
Radiations, ionising, 115
  blood disease from, 117
  pre-natal exposure, 132
Radiation sickness, 117
Radioactive dust, 115
  paints, 120
Rats, black, as plague carriers, 5–6
Respiratory infections, control, 79
Rhesus babies, 130, 133
  factor, 103
Rhizopoda, 63
Rickettsia, 53, 62
Rodents, hosts of plague, 5

Salmonellae, 45
Scarlet fever, 44
Schick test, 88–9
Schistosomiasis, 72
Septicaemia, 44, 46
Serum sickness, 100
Shigellae, 45
Shingles, 60
Silicosis, 110
Skin grafting, immunology, 107
Slate, silicosis from, 111
Sleeping sickness (*see* Trypanosomiasis)
Smallpox, 59
  distribution, 11, 12
Smog, 108
Smoking, 122
Snow, Dr John, 13
Soil erosion, 150
Spastic paralysis, 126
Staphylococcus, 40, 46
Streptococcus, 40, 44
Streptomycin, 92, 94
Sulphonamides, 6, 27, 91
  mode of action, 92
Syphilis, 47, 49
  congenital, 49–50

Tape worms, 71, 73
Terramycin, 92
Tetanus, 43
Thailand project, 35
Thalidomide, 131
Thymus, in immunity, 107

Tobacco mosaic virus, 52
Tonsillitis, 41, 44
Toxins, 41
  classification, 42
Toxoids, 87
Trachoma, 25
  distribution, 25, 26
  virus, 55, 56
Translocation of chromosomes, 129
Trematoda, 71
Treponema pallidum, 47
  pertenue, 49
Treponematoses, 47
  distribution, 48
  penicillin treatment, 94
Trypanosomes, 67
Trypanosoma cruzi, 67
  gambiense, 67
  rhodesiense, 67
Trypanosomiasis, 24, 67
Tse-tse fly, 24
Tuberculin test, 90, 100
Tuberculosis, 46
  control, 89
Tumours, viral, 61
Typhoid, 45
Typhus (*see also* Rickettsia), 53
  endemic, 62
  in World Wars, 8

UNDERNOURISHMENT, 136
United Nations International Children's Emergency Fund (U.N.I.C.E.F.), 33
United Nations Relief and Rehabilitation Administration (U.N.R.R.A.), 33

VACCINATION, 10
Vaccines, 86
Valmer patch test, 90
Van Pinguet test, 90
Venereal disease, control, 79
Vibrio cholerae, 44
Viruses, 38, 50
  and cancer, 61
  effect on foetus, 132
  entry of, 54
  interferon, 97–8
  invasion patterns, 56
  laboratory culture, 53
  make-up of, 52
  sizes of, 51

WAR, and typhus, 7, 8
Water-borne diseases, control, 78
Whooping cough, 44
World Health Organisation (W.H.O.), 1, 6, 12, 27
  history of, 30
  and malaria, 34
Worms, parasitic, 68, 70

YAWS, 49, 50
Yellow fever, 18
  distribution, 19, 20